Their Tangled Hearts

Mary DeWeber

Prepared for publication by Steven Long

Consultant editor Amanda Long

ISBN-13: 978-0692232293
ISBN-10: 069223229X

CONTENTS

Chapter 1

Emma drew a deep breath and flexed her shoulders in an attempt to relieve the stiffness in the tense muscles of her neck and back. The late April breeze coming in the open windows felt like silk against her skin as it ruffled her shoulder length honey blonde hair. She had been driving for almost two hours. Towing a small-enclosed trailer over the Rocky Mountains was a new experience for her. The pass had proved to be a challenge, but she had taken it slow and hadn't had any major problems. For the last half hour she had been driving along a narrow road that wound over wooded hills and past stately pines following the signs pointing to the Lazy J Ranch.

She should have known better than to have lunch with her guardian, Doc Linden, last week. It seemed that he was always talking her into something. She shook her head as she remembered how he had manipulated her into this latest escapade.

"Come on Em, Joe and Sue Jacobs need you," he'd pleaded. "They're already short staffed and they're having a rough time finding someone willing to take on a temporary job, cooking and helping out on a cattle ranch. Just stay while Sue's laid up for the next six weeks or so. I'm sure they can find another helper in that amount of time."

"Doc, is this another of your schemes to 'draw me out'?" She asked suspiciously. "Like the Job Corps, the game preserve, the homeless shelter etc... I'm perfectly happy as I am."

"No Em," he sighed. There was deep sadness in his pale blue eyes as he looked at the tall, too thin woman in front of him,

"You haven't been truly happy for the past five years. Don't forget I've known you since birth and you're a pale imitation of the person you once were."

"People change. No one stays the same for the rest of their life."

"Not this kind of change. You've been hit with blow after blow, far more than most people can handle." He broke off with a grimace. "Just look at you, sitting there so tense you couldn't possibly relax if you wanted to. You've buried your emotions so deep that love could walk up and slap you in the face and you'd never know it. You've stretched yourself to the breaking point. I haven't even seen you smile in ages."

"Let me finish," he continued as she shook her head and opened her mouth in denial. "You know I'm talking about your real smile, the one that is so infectious it brightens the whole room and makes everyone want to smile with you," he added gruffly.

"You used to be so full of life, and now…"

"Look Doc," she interjected wearily, with a raised hand. "I've heard all this before. I know you want the best for me, but I've got to deal with this my own way. I just can't take any more pain, not now, maybe not ever."

With tears in his eyes he accepted her words, but still his heart cried out for the warm loving woman she had once been. "Some day Carl will get what's coming to him," he muttered.

Emma eyed him with eyes that had gone as cold and gray as the North Sea. "I've asked you not to speak that name."

"I'm sorry Em, but I can't help wanting to throttle the man who has turned you into the ghost of the woman you used to be."

"You and me both." She agreed with a forced smile.

"Okay honey," he sighed. "I'll call Joe and tell him I'll keep looking for a replacement."

"You old fraud." She smiled stiffly. "You know I'll go, but what about my work?"

"You'll have a cabin to yourself with plenty of peace and quiet. Just take along your equipment."

"I intend to, but I'll need privacy to work. Do they know what I do?"

"I told them you work for a sound studio."

"Thanks, you know I don't want anyone to knowing about my songwriting. People don't understand how grueling the work is and they can make my life difficult."

"Your life has been difficult enough."

"Then quit trying to complicate it even more. I mean it Doc, this is the last time I'll let you volunteer me for anything."

"We'll see," he'd smiled.

Coming out of her reverie Emma swerved to miss a large rock in the road. Too late! It caught her driver side rear tire. Great! A flat tire was not what she needed at this point. She sighed. The tools were, of course, underneath everything in the trunk and it took a while to dig them out with the spare tire.

She'd just finished reading the instructions on the jack, when she heard a vehicle approaching. Gripping the tire iron she turned as a white pick-up truck with the now familiar Lazy J symbol printed on the side came into view. The knot of fear in her stomach eased at the sight of a woman's friendly face.

"Hi there! You must be Emma Winters," the smiling brunette called out, taking in the loaded car and trailer. "I'm Sue Jacobs and this is my husband Joe."

"I'm pleased to meet you Mr. and Mrs. Jacobs." Emma motioned to the tools spread out beside the car, and continued. "I wanted to be early, but I'm afraid that I had a flat tire."

"No problem," Joe smiled as he got out of the truck, and with an ease that amazed Emma, made short work of changing the flat.

"Please, call us Joe and Sue. We are quite informal at the ranch." The petite woman with an engaging grin held out her hand. "It will be so good to have another woman on the place again. Although, I must admit that men are good to have around sometimes," she motioned to her husband.

"I agree, there are times when they come in handy. I haven't changed many tires."

"We were glad when Doc told us you would help us out. What did he tell you about the situation here? I suppose he made it sound like I'm on my last leg." She chuckled at her own joke as she motioned to the crutches at her side. "I took a bad fall and broke my ankle two weeks ago. I still have another five weeks before the cast comes off and I'm up and around."

"He just said you are short staffed and need help. I'm willing to do whatever is needed. It must be frustrating being bound to crutches."

"Don't waste too much pity on her." Joe smiled. "She rules us all with an iron fist."

"In a velvet glove?" Sue laughed and blew a kiss at her tall sandy haired husband. "Don't go frightening Emma off already, we need her." The banter continued as Joe stored the tools into the back of Emma's car and repacked the trunk.

As she followed the pick-up to the ranch Emma reflected on her new employers. They were friendly and seemed to have a terrific relationship. Sighing, she knew a relationship was something she would never have. When you let someone get too close you got hurt, and her scars ran far too deep to let anyone hurt her again.

The Lazy J Ranch was nestled among the trees at the base of the Rocky Mountains. The main building, which housed offices and living quarters, was built of peeled logs. A long porch furnished with white painted rocking chairs and inviting porch swings ran the length of the building. Rustic cabins had been scattered invitingly throughout the trees with enough space and undergrowth between them to afford a small amount of privacy. They pulled to a stop at the last, most secluded, cabin.

The log structure with its steeply pitched, green metal roof and shutters, seemed to nestle comfortably into the trees. The covered porch with its pair of rocking chairs and small table beckoned invitingly.

Sue maneuvered her crutches up the stairs, and unlocked the front door. Then, handing Emma the key, she led the way into the main room of the cabin. It was decorated in earthy tones with a decidedly southwest flair, spartan yet tasteful. Definitely a mans room.

"I hope this will suit you. The bedroom and bathroom are through that door. Doc told us you do some kind of sound work and there is a sound proof room over here. My brother Jake had it built before he was married."

"This is perfect; the sound proofing will go a long way toward keeping peace with your guests. I do a lot of work at night, and I prefer not to wear headphones if I can help it. My equipment's out in the trailer, it will be nice to have a good place to put it."

"We aren't taking guests at this time. There are five ranch hands in the bunkhouse and Ken our stable boss and my brother Jake are in two of the other cabins, but I doubt anyone could hear you unless you hook speakers up outside," Sue smiled.

Joe put his head around the door and announced the arrival of the ranch hands to help unload the trailer.

An hour and a half later with everything unloaded, Emma went to the main building, in search of Sue. Coming through the front door, her breath caught in wonder. The room opening beyond the office foyer was lovely. A long bar at the right served as the main desk, but her attention was caught by the floor to ceiling windows on the opposite wall. Her gaze was drawn past the flagstone terrace to a small river flowing through the gentle valley that sloped up to snow covered peaks. Steps led down into the main room, or great room of the lodge, the center of which showcased a large round fireplace made of rugged stone. The whole effect spoke of cozy evenings curled up in one of the comfortable chairs or love seats, which were arranged in casual groups around the room. Massive wood beams supported the peak ceiling and white painted walls gave the area a sense of light and space. The polished wood floor was scattered with rugs in muted tones in keeping with the southwestern decor. The setting reminded her of a weekend she had once spent at an upscale ski resort in Vail.

"It kind of gets to you doesn't it?"

Startled, Emma turned, and saw Sue sitting in one of the chairs with her leg propped on an ottoman. She had obviously been working on the paperwork, which was scattered across a low table.

"Come have a seat. You must be bursting with questions," Sue smiled invitingly, and gestured to a nearby, overstuffed chair.

Emma could feel the tension slowly easing from her as she crossed the room. Maybe Doc was right; she had been working too hard these past months. The restful atmosphere of the ranch might be just what she needed.

"Doc didn't tell me much about the job. He only said that you were short staffed, and need someone to cook and help out."

"Well, he was right about that, we recently lost our main helper when his family moved to the city. We need someone to help with the children who come in a couple times a week for horseback riding, it's not difficult, but safety is of utmost importance. Joe will explain all of that to you tomorrow."

Sue gestured ruefully. "I hate to ask you to help me with meals, but for the past week Joe have been my main helper and the food is awful. My husband may be a wonder at running a ranch, but he's a total loss in the kitchen," she grinned

"I came ready to do whatever is needed." Emma reassured her. "What about cleaning?"

"A local woman comes in during the week which helps. I run the office and do the bookkeeping," she said with a grimace, motioning to the paperwork.

Emma protested when Sue named a generous salary in addition to room and board. Sue quickly pointed out that Emma wouldn't have set working hours and would, pretty much, be on call.

"How would you like a tour of the building?"

"I'd love it. That is if you're feeling up to it, of course." Emma glanced at her in concern. "We could always postpone it if you wish."

"There's no time like the present. I can't stand being bound down for too long. I haven't been this still for," Sue grinned as she rose gracefully to her feet, "well... I don't remember how long. That's why I like to do as much of the office work as possible out here, where I can at least, see the mountains, even though I'd prefer to be out on a horse or helping with the children."

"Joe's parents originally designed this place as a guest ranch and they added the cattle as they could afford it. We have two hundred and sixty acres of working ranch, and also run cattle on the open range belonging to the forest service. The cattle eat the underbrush, which helps keep the fire danger to a minimum. So you can see, the ranch hands have all they can handle and don't have time to help around the lodge."

"You mentioned earlier, that you aren't taking regular guests at this time. Do you have any plans to re-open the lodge?" Emma gestured around the room. "I'm sure there are a lot of people who would be interested in staying here."

"We still occasionally take a few established guests, but we are getting away from being a traditional guest ranch. Eventually, we want to have a Christian camp for the families of disabled children. A place they can come, where the special needs children won't be treated any different than their siblings. Often, when there is a handicapped child in the family, the other children suffer. It takes so much time and energy to care for them that the others get overlooked. There are quite a few good programs out there already, that are willing to help a child with disabilities, but there aren't many who are willing to take on the rest of the family."

Sue, busy negotiating the stairs with her crutches had missed Emma's shock at the mention of disabled children. Surely Doc wouldn't do that to her. For a moment Emma fought the blind panic that washed over her when Sue mentioned their plans for the ranch. Slowly her heartbeat returned to normal when she realized that Sue was talking about future plans. With great effort, Emma forced her attention back to what Sue was saying before she noticed the change in her.

"It won't be easy and we'll need a lot of staff. The children will have a strict schedule of meals, swimming, horseback riding, and other activities specific to their abilities. We will need a one on one counselor to work with the severely handicapped children during the day. I think it would be good to incorporate the non-handicapped children into the same activities as their siblings. You would be surprised how many of them help with the daily care of their brothers or sisters. The kids can have fun while their parents get a chance to enjoy our adult amenities."

Sue motioned excitedly out the windows pointing out where they wanted to make improvements. "Of course, we'll have to make the cabins wheelchair accessible, and the addition of an enclosed arena, gym, pool, and sauna will expand our scope of care. I have a degree in business and Joe recently finished his Masters degrees in sociology and physical therapy. He was a counselor at a Christian camp when we met. We know that when the time is right, God will help us put it all together."

Her pretty face was flushed, and her dark eyes

shone as she spoke, and for a moment Emma envied the fire she saw in Sue's eyes. Emma could easily see the enormous amount of energy that would be needed to carry out such plans.

"I'm sorry; I know I get carried away. I'm just so frustrated that I can't do more," Sue laughed. "Joe says I have too much time on my hands to think these days!"

As they spoke, they had been slowly moving down the hall behind the check-in desk. "Here are the offices, supply rooms and laundry, feel free to use the facilities any time you want." After a quick inspection they returned to the reception area and crossed to a door marked 'private'.

"This is our living quarters," Sue said leading the way into a tastefully decorated sitting room. Pillows in assorted shades of burgundy and rose were piled on the deep leather sofa and chairs, which were grouped around a large entertainment center with television and stereo equipment. The room was warm and rich, reflecting the inner beauty of the woman herself.

"There are four bedrooms back there and a small kitchen, though we eat all our meals in the main dining room."

"The other end of the building is where you'll be spending a lot of time. Thankfully we don't have many clients yet this year."

Moving back into the reception area. Sue deftly led

the way down the steps and to the right, across the great room. They passed through an arch set in the far wall and entered the dining room.

Floor to ceiling windows and double doors opening onto the terrace, made the most of the fantastic view. Whoever decorated the lodge had continued the tasteful southwestern décor of the great room, throughout the dining area. Emma could see that the room would hold a substantial amount of guests, even though it was obvious that only one end was in use.

They made their way toward the kitchen doors as Sue explained the present serving procedure. "The men pick up the food as they pass through the kitchen and bring it to the table. You aren't here to be a waitress. I'll help you with any preparation work I can do while sitting down and you'll have help with the dishes."

Emma passed through the double swinging doors and came to a halt, staring open-mouthed, at the gleaming kitchen. Stainless steel cabinets and work surfaces shone with the effort of much polishing. A commercial range with six burners sat near the gleaming grill, while double ovens sent forth a heavenly aroma.

Sue's wide smile expressed delight at the shock registering on Emma's face. "Don't you just adore it?" She cried. "I know it looks intimidating, but, it's so easy to work in here. There is a walk in refrigerator over there and the deep freeze units are here. And this..." She said with a flourish. "Is the dish room."

Standing aside she waved Emma into a room filled with a large commercial dishwasher and lined with a counter, sinks, and shelves.

"Wow," breathed Emma. "This is a dream kitchen."

"It's all necessary for commercial foodservice and I absolutely love it. It's taken a lot of remodeling to bring it up to health code," Sue sighed happily.

"Is that wonderful aroma I smell a pot roast? I thought you said the food has been awful."

"One dish dinners are currently my specialty. As long as I can sit on a stool with my foot up, I can sort of cook, but I can't do it all." Sue sat down at a table in the corner of the kitchen. "Got any questions?"

"A few. For starters, how many people do I prepare for? When are the meals, and what time do I need to be here in the morning?" Emma ticked the questions off on her fingers.

"You'll be cooking for ten people including yourself, but I always make extra." Sue grinned. "It seems like, there is always someone raiding the kitchen."

They spent the afternoon working out schedules and menus and before long it was time to start the remainder of the supper. The women worked well together. Emma tried to anticipate what Sue would need so she wouldn't feel helpless.

By the time the men appeared there were platters of succulent roast beef with vegetables and gravy. Bowls of fresh green salad and yeast rolls hot from the oven. Dessert was apple cobbler with ice cream.

After Joe said grace, the hungry men dove into the feast, quickly devouring the food at an alarming rate.

Ken, the stable boss, who was a small, wizened man of about sixty years old, finally pushed away from the table with a blissful sigh. "You better not keep feeding us like this Miss. Emma or we'll all grow fat and lazy." This elicited a shout of laughter from the crowd as they lingered over their coffee.

A tall slender young man Emma identified as Slim crowed. "Won't Romeo be madder'n a wet hen when he finds out what he's missed? He and Jake won't be back till mornin'."

"That will be soon enough," registered Joe. "I wanted Miss Emma to get settled before subjecting her to Romeo." Turning to Emma he explained, "Romeo isn't a bad sort he's just a bit of a flirt."

Emma looked around sharply. "We'll get along fine, as long as he leaves me alone." For some reason, the men thought this an extremely funny remark, and on that note they rose and quickly cleared the table amidst a rash of good-natured banter.

Joe helped with the dishes that night and they made short work of the task. Then Emma bid goodnight to her new employer and returned to her cabin.

*   *   *

Sue looked up as Joe walked through the door of their apartment.

"How did it go?"

"Fine. Emma seems to know her way around a kitchen." Joe settled onto the couch next to his wife.

"I noticed that earlier. Did you let Doc know that she made it here in one piece?"

"Yes, I called him after we finished unloading the trailer. She has a lot of sophisticated equipment. From what I could see, she'll have a pretty good recording studio when she gets it all set up."

"Doc only mentioned that she worked independently, for a sound studio."

I asked him about her, but he just said that Emma's story wasn't his to tell."

"Don't you think it's a little suspicious, that he should send us someone who works in the music industry?" Sue adjusted her foot on the ottoman.

"Doc knows what he's doing. Who knows? Maybe this will shake up that brother of yours."

"Jake needs something to shake him out of the rut

he's settled into."

"I have a feeling Emma is going to shake up a lot of things around here," Joe said thoughtfully. "Did you notice her reaction to Slims ribbing?"

"Did I ever. What else did Doc tell you about her?"

"Just that she's been through a rough time, and needs a lot of prayer."

Sue's dark eyes glowed. "Well, prayer is one thing we can do in abundance." They joined hands and bowed their heads.

*   *   *

Emma surveyed her equipment. The men had placed it in the sound room, and it seemed to have made the move without any damage. She had carefully packed each piece herself and was more than a little nervous when the men had started unloading the trailer.

With great care she began to assemble her studio. Finding a good set up of electrical outlets made the job easier than expected and in record time she was ready for a sound check.

Over the course of the day Sue had made a comment about timing that stuck with her, tickling her conscious mind, and bringing a snippet of melody with it, that had teased her elusively all evening long. She let her fingers play over the keys and before long a tender love song flowed forth. Emma recorded the basic song. Then came the real work of adding harmonies, and filling in the music with extra tracks from her synthesizer. The finished project sounded as if an entire band were playing with her. After writing the title and the name of a well-known popular singing artist on the CD, she placed it with the sheet music she had tediously filled out on a shelf, and glanced at the clock. Two a.m., maybe now she could get some sleep.

As she tumbled into bed she thought fleetingly of the 'gift' in her life. For as long as she could remember, music had been a big part of her. As a child her parents had encouraged her to sing, recording the songs she made up and playing them for friends. In junior high school, her choir teacher had sent a demo tape to a music producer who had been his roommate in college. Emma knew that without his endorsement, Greg Paulson would never have listened to her music, let alone recognized her potential. Soon she was making good money as her songs rose quickly to the top of the charts. She invested in more sophisticated equipment and started turning out high quality recordings. The sudden death of her parents when she was sixteen had brought a new depth and maturity to her music.

Dr. Hal Linden and his wife Martha had been good friends of the family for years. They were childless and had been thrilled when Ted and Emily Winters asked them to be Emma's godparents. When the car accident claimed Ted and Emily's lives, 'Doc' and Martha had stepped in and become her guardians.

Doc and Martha had always encouraged Emma's

music. It came as no surprise to them that the songs not only came to her with words and melody, but with all the background music and the voice of a specific performer in her head. When Emma was a girl, she was quite often moody, and her teachers thought there was something wrong with her. They didn't understand how music controlled her mood swings. She was sensitive to such a point, that she became caught up in whatever emotion the music portrayed. Happiness, joy, love, anger or melancholy flowed through her in abundance every time she heard music playing, or 'heard' it in her head. It had taken her a long time and a lot of patience, to be able to properly control her feelings and to know how to handle them. In recent years she had fine-tuned her control to the point where she could put up a wall and hide her emotions from everyone.

Well, almost everyone, she conceded as Doc's face flashed through her mind. Doc could always see right through her. He seemed to understand what she was going through even when she was a child. He had been fiercely protective of her in her professional dealings with Greg, and he carefully went over every contract and had his lawyer make sure she was protected. Doc had even went to bat for her when Greg balked at passing her songs along to other artists, regardless of his own opinions of who would be best for them.

Greg quickly learned to give the demo directly to the artist Emma suggested or it would flop long before making it to the charts.

It was Greg who had encouraged her to write under a pseudonym to keep her life private, at least until she was older. At first he hadn't liked the idea of sharing her music with artists his company didn't represent, but the money she made him quickly changed his mind. Soon Jeri Forester's songs were greeted with open arms in all areas of the music industry.

In college, she joined a band and began to sing for dances and gatherings. Soon they'd had steady work in nightclubs, and at parties. She was careful to only do songs that a recording artist had already made popular and she kept her identity a secret, even from her closest friends.

Emma yawned, the strain of the day finally caught up with her and though exhausted, she fell into a fitful sleep.

Chapter 2

There was a great heaviness in Emma's limbs, she couldn't run she tried to fight but the pressure was holding her down. Her screams rent the night as she fought the numbing terror that, once again, held her within its icy grip. There was something, someone pressing her down, hurting her, touching... A pounding noise filtered through her consciousness. Her bedroom door burst open bringing her suddenly awake. Struggling into a sitting position, she blinked at the bright light flooding the room and momentarily blinding her. A dark, mountain of a man came through the door and reached for her. She threw her hands up to ward him off as another terrified scream ripped through the quiet of the night.

"It's all right, I'm not going to hurt you, I'm here, I'm here," soothed a voice as warm and comforting as velvet.

Emma struggled wildly. Lashing out her fist connected with his cheekbone. He easily caught both her wrists in one large hand and pulled her into his arms. The stranger held her with a curious combination of strength and gentleness as he soothed her.

The words he uttered didn't register at first, but the warm voice seeping through her consciousness like a comforting balm, was somehow slightly familiar. When she finally realized he would not hurt her she stopped struggling. He released her wrists and drew her into his embrace where she clung convulsively to him. Her face, resting against his broad flannel covered chest was wet with tears as her anguished sobs racked her body. His strong arms held her trembling form as she fought to bring her breathing slowly under control.

The man held her as if she were a frightened child and she, in her confused state, allowed herself, for the first time in many years, to draw comfort from another individual.

At last, when the reality of the situation dawned upon her, she was suddenly embarrassed. She drew a shaky breath and pulled back to look up into the darkest eyes she had ever seen.

Startled by the deep concern Emma saw in their depths, she pulled away stammering, "I'm s-so sorry."

"Don't be," the man smiled. "Do you have nightmares often?"

"They're not usually this bad." Suddenly cold, she shivered and clutched the blanket to her chest. Confusion colored her voice as she asked. "How-?"

"I came in late last night and couldn't sleep. I was on my front porch waiting for sunrise when I heard you scream." Smiling he held up his hands. "It's a good thing I still have the key or I'm afraid I would have broken the door down."

While he spoke he got up from the side of the bed and moved to a chair. For the first time she saw he was wearing an open jacket and flannel shirt. No wonder he had felt so warm and comforting.

"You must be Emma. I heard about you from Sue, when I called last evening to see if she needed anything from town before I headed out."

She realized that he'd deliberately been talking to give her some much-needed breathing space, in which to gather her wits.

When he reached out his hand, Emma didn't hesitate to place hers into it. "I'm Sue's brother Jake Peterson," he introduced himself formally, as he politely shook her hand.

"It's nice to meet you," she said automatically. "I'm Emma Winters."

As Emma sat looking up at him, she was suddenly struck by the absurdity of the situation. A bubble of nervous laughter welled up from some secret place deep inside and surprised her by escaping.

Jake, determining she was not hysterical, grinned and soon they were both laughing.

Emma quickly gained control. Laughter frightened her; it had been so long since she had loosened the reigns of her feelings enough to laugh like that. She

l

felt emotionally exposed in a way she hadn't
allowed herself to be for a very long time.

Sensing the change in her Jake asked, "Are you
going to be alright now?"

"Yes I'll be fine, thank you."

"No more nightmares?"

"No more," she promised.

"Well I'd better go then. I'm glad we've met,
Emma Winters. If you need me again just scream,"
he said with a smile and was gone. The front door
closed quietly as he went out. Inexplicably, the
room seemed suddenly empty without his presence.

"There's no sense in sitting here brooding. I might
as well get up," she told herself glancing at the
clock. It was still early but she couldn't stay in bed
any longer.

Standing under the shower she thought about the
nightmare. Every time she was under heavy stress,
the nightmares surfaced. Painful memories flooded
her as she relived the night five years ago that still
continued to haunt her.

Her band had finished up for the night. They'd
played at a party downtown and her car had balked
at starting. The others, not realizing she was having
trouble had already left. The battery on her cell
phone was dead and she was just heading inside for
a telephone when a well-dressed man walked from
the building. She had seen him watching her on

stage, but that was to be expected, so she hadn't thought much about it. During her breaks he had singled her out and they'd talked. He said his name was Carl Robertson, he'd seemed nice and he was very flattering. She had noticed his blond good looks and the deep dimple in his left cheek. What she hadn't noticed was how much he'd been drinking. When he approached her in the parking lot and offered her a ride home she had, with the innocence of youth, accepted.

When they reached her apartment he'd made a show of looking at his cell and complaining of a dead battery he asked to use her phone. Once inside her apartment he began to flirt with her. Aware that she was in a difficult situation, she had tried to humor him and let him kiss her goodnight, but his breath had been heavy with alcohol and she had been repulsed. When she'd tried to pull away, he'd ignored her protests and began pushing things too far. She told him to leave, but he wouldn't listen. That was when things had gotten ugly.

She hadn't called the police. Her shame was so great that she didn't want to face anyone. She'd hidden most of the bruises and made up a story about having tripped in the dark to explain away her bruised cheek and split lip.

Over and over, she had asked herself, why God let this happen to her. Was it some kind of punishment? Why did she have to live her life in what amounted to an emotional vacuum, afraid of being hurt again? The unanswered questions chased each other around in her head like a squirrel in a cage.

The water in the shower had gone as cold as her heart and as she turning off the taps, she once again closed the door on the memories that had surfaced.

Quickly Emma shivered into her clothes and blow-dried her hair, pulling it back into its customary ponytail. She studied her reflection in the mirror. Thick, shoulder length honey brown hair, curled rebelliously from the confines of the elastic band. There were dark smudges under the thick-fringed gray eyes that for too long hadn't seen the blue green sparks that showed through when she smiled. Her face was pale and drawn, lending an air of fragility to her thin, five foot seven inch frame. At twenty-seven she was less worried about fashion then she was comfort. Jeans and baggy T-shirts were the mainstays of her wardrobe, though she had brought a few dressier outfits, as she hadn't been sure what was expected of her. For some unknown reason she felt a vague sense of dissatisfaction with her looks. Impatiently she shrugged into her jacket and set off for the kitchen. As she walked past Jake's cabin, she failed to notice him sitting in the shadows of his porch, keeping watch over her.

Emma threw herself into breakfast preparations. Her years working with the Job Corps and other causes Doc had talked her into, now stood her in good stead. Hard work had always helped her to keep unwanted thoughts at bay, but every time she remembered her nightmare she burned with embarrassment. What had Jake told Joe and Sue about the incident? Probably that they had hired a psychotic woman.

When Sue came into the kitchen on her crutches, she gasped. "Oh my goodness, I can't believe I overslept." Stopping in her tracks she whistled, "Whew, what a spread!" She sank onto her stool and accepted the cup of coffee Emma handed her. "You must have been up before dawn to have done all this." Sue marveled.

"I'm an early riser," Emma gave a small smile as she tucked a stray curl behind her ear.

"I'm not a morning person," Sue grinned. "That's why breakfast isn't any earlier. If the guys would let me get away with it I'd tell them all to eat cereal and let me sleep."

"I don't mind doing breakfast alone, if you'd like."

"You've just became my favorite person in the whole world." Sue enthused.

"Anyone who'll let you sleep in is your favorite person." Jake's velvety voice entered the room with him. "Morning Susie."

"Hey stranger, when did you get in?" she asked, while ducking her head to get away as her brother playfully tousled her long dark hair.

"About two this morning. Everything was quiet so I didn't bother you."

"Well, how in the world did you get that shiner?" Sue asked in concern.

"I ran into an immovable object." He dodged as looked over at Emma. "This must be Miss Emma the boys have been raving about." He smiled a friendly greeting and since he failed to bring up their earlier meeting, she was inclined not to mention it either.

"Jake this is Emma Winters, our new cook and helper. You have her to thank for all of this." Sue waved her hand expansively at the spread of food before them. "Emma this is my clumsy brother, Jake Peterson."

"It's nice to meet you Mr. Peterson," said Emma as she once again shook hands with him.

"Jake will do. We don't stand much on ceremony around here." There was a twinkle in his dark eyes and the right side of his mouth twitched as if he were trying not to smile.

Emma once again heard that elusive familiarity in his voice, but she couldn't quite pin it down. Perhaps she was still suffering from the after effects of her nightmare. Suddenly conscious, that he was still holding her hand, she pulled back nervously rubbing her hands together.

Sue glanced from one to the other, wondering at Emma's faintly pink cheeks.

"Well, well, what have we here?" Drawled a voice

from the doorway. A well-built man in his late twenties leaned against the doorjamb.

Emma blanched, almost causing the smudge of flour on her right cheek to disappear. This must be the man Slim had referred to as Romeo. He would have been handsome, had it not been for the self assured smirk on his tanned features. When he straightened and swaggered into the room, Emma had the urge to step behind Jake, but stood her ground. As he drew closer she realized that although he put on a powerful image, he was really a couple of inches shorter than she was. She recognized the look in his eyes; she had seen it many times before.

In the past, she would have regarded the situation with amusement, but not now. There was a distinct wariness about her as she acknowledged this newcomer who, not surprisingly, reminded her of a banty rooster.

Sue thrust a platter of food in Romeo's hands as he approached. "Romeo, this is Emma, she is responsible for this lovely breakfast."

"It sure is good to meet you Miss. Emma." Romeo grinned with a cocky air.

Emma stiffly murmured an appropriate response. She was spared further contact by the arrival of the remainder of the men.

Slim, at the head of the pack, paused dramatically, sniffed the air and announced, "Boys we've died and gone to heaven!"

With a whoop the 'boys' scooped up the serving dishes laden with hot biscuits, sausage gravy, fluffy scrambled eggs, hashed browned potatoes and crispy bacon and disappeared through the swinging doors. Thankful for the diversion, Emma breathed a sigh of relief.

"Saved by the bell," Sue muttered, as she followed them into the dining room.

Emma breathed a sigh of relief and joined them. She couldn't help but notice the easy camaraderie the men shared, as they joined together to make her workload light.

Jake covertly watched Emma during the meal, worried over the change he had seen in her at the entrance of Romeo. He remembered the full-throated terror he had heard in her screams as he sat on his porch this morning. Not knowing what he would find when he burst into the cabin, he was startled to see a terrified woman in what had once been his bed. He'd instinctively, treated her no differently than he had treated his daughter, Candy, when she had awakened with a bad dream so long ago. This however, was not a child's dream. This was something dark and alarming. Something, he realized, he would do anything to take away.

Emma had an indefinable strength of will that showed in the tilt of her head and the way she had drawn herself up to her full height when confronted by Romeo. This morning, in her cabin, he'd noticed that she had pulled herself together, when he could tell she wanted to lean in and draw on his strength for a while longer. She was not a small woman, but her delicate features and the dark circles under her eyes added to the fragile air about her. He hadn't wanted to protect someone like this since losing Amy and Candy to the icy roads three years ago. That had been a bad time in his life and he realized that without God's grace, he undoubtedly would have become a bitter and disillusioned man.

As he watched, Emma rose to fetch the jam from the kitchen. When she passed by Romeo's chair he snaked an arm out and encircled her waist.

"Why don't we forget this bunch and you and me can cook up something special, just the two of us?" Romeo drawled.

In the shocked silence that followed the remark, Jake saw a momentary look of revulsion flash across Emma's face before she pasted on a brittle smile and spoke in an icy tone.

"Mr. Romeo, unless you want 'finger' sandwiches for lunch, I'd advise you to keep your hands to yourself!" Disengaging his arm she sailed, head high, into the kitchen amidst cheers.

"Haw, haw, that'll teach you!" Laughed Slim.

Returning with the jam, a white faced Emma gave Romeo a wide berth.

Jake let out the breath he had been unconsciously

holding since the moment Romeo reached for her. The blood pounded painfully in his ears and he fought to control his desire to throttle the man. This wasn't the first time he had found Romeo's behavior less than palatable. Why Joe kept the man on was beyond him. He would definitely have a talk with Romeo later.

Joe rose to his feet. "Listen up guys," he spoke with a stern look around the table. "Miss Emma came here as a favor to help us out and I for one don't want to lose her. You will all mind your manners and treat her with the same consideration you would your own sister, understand?" At the murmurs of assent he went right into their various assignments.

As Emma listened to the day's instructions she mentally thanked Joe for his decisive handling of an unpleasant situation. Scanning the faces at the table she was impressed by what she saw. The men, with the exception of Romeo, were truly wonderful. They were warm and polite with a mixture of boyish enthusiasm and Old World charm. She thought of her momentary panic when Romeo had reached for her. The feeling she had received from the room in general was that any and all of the men would immediately have jumped to her rescue. The sensation surprised her and filled her with unfamiliar warmth. She had seen the tension on Jake's face and knew that she had to act fast. She had rushed into her spiel about finger sandwiches for fear of what may ensue. She certainly didn't want to cause trouble for these kind people and would be more cautious in the future.

Sue had said something about her cabin having been Jake's before he got married and Emma wondered when she would meet his wife. For some reason she couldn't put her finger on, the thought depressed her. The memory of his strong arms had stayed with her. Male contact was something she usually found repulsive, but she had felt safe and protected while clinging to him. Pulling her thoughts up short she chided herself for not paying more attention to Joe. She rose to help clear the table amidst shy comments and heartfelt thanks from the 'boys'.

Jake, it seemed, was the resident dishwasher. They worked companionably together for a while before Emma worked up enough courage to bring up the subject of his early morning 'rescue'.

"Thanks for not mentioning this morning to anyone." Emma said quietly. "And, did I give you that black eye?" she asked.

"Well, you do pack quite a wallop!" he grinned. Then he sobered. "I'm sorry about that scene with Romeo; you shouldn't have to put up with that sort of thing. You certainly put him in his place."

"I'm not worried about Romeo. I've met men like him before," she said with disdain. "I've used that line before when I worked in a night club. It gets the point across."

"You don't seem like the type to work in a club." Jake smiled.

"That was my wild youth," she quickly changed the

subject. "Sue mentioned that my cabin was yours before you married. Is that why you have a key?"

"Yes, it was mine," there was a shadow in his eyes as he spoke. "This morning was the first time I've been there since before the car accident that killed my wife and daughter three years ago."

"I'm so sorry," Emma murmured, her eyes darkened to a deep blue gray, and she laid her hand on his arm. "It seems like I'm always saying that. My parents died the same way. I know it doesn't help, but I truly am sorry." Embarrassed by her momentary lapse of control she turned her head and pulled her hand away to wipe out the sink. What in the world was the matter with her?

"Thank-you," the two words spoken softy and fraught with so much feeling, had more impact than a lengthy speech. "That's not why you have nightmares though, is it?" Emma stiffened and he silently chastised himself for once again causing her to close herself off.

"No." She walked away and wiped the end of the counter.

Wanting to keep her talking Jake grasped at the first thought that came into his head. "I don't want you to feel uncomfortable knowing I have a key to your cabin. I'd be happy to give it to you, if it would make you feel better. "

Emma considered this for a moment. For some reason she didn't understand she felt...safer, knowing he would be there in an instant if she needed him. Instinctively she knew she could trust him. That he would never hurt her.

"Maybe you should keep it," she said as she hung up her apron and smiled thoughtfully. If she was going to be working with children she should probably try to lighten up some. "I wouldn't want to be the cause of a broken door or another black eye."

With that, she made a show of dusting her hands. "Thanks for your help. Now, can you point me to the stable?"

"Sure, but, you might want to wipe that smudge of flour off your face first."

"What, where?" She blushed and scrubbed at her face. "How long has that been there?"

"All morning," he grinned.

"So much for a girl's vanity," she grinned ruefully. "Come on, our first client will be here soon and I want to acquaint myself with the procedures."

With a laugh, Jake followed her out of the kitchen.

Joe met them at the stable. "We have two kids today Jody, and Gracie. Jody was born with spinal bifida and Gracie lost a leg to bone cancer. This is the harness they will wear while riding." He went on explaining the procedure, but Emma was no longer listening.

Disabled kids...Sue had said disabled kids but

Emma had thought she meant some time in the future, not now. Surely not now.

With great effort she tried to hear what Joe was saying. How could Doc do this to her?

There was a hand on her arm leading her to a bench. A voice pierced the sound of blood rushing in her ears. "Sit here and put your head between your knees before you faint. Didn't you eat any breakfast?" After a moment her head cleared and Emma looked up into the concerned faces hovering over her.

"I'm sorry-"

"Stop apologizing," Jake cut in. "Sit there a minute you're white as a sheet." Emma leaned her head back against the wall and took a deep breath. "As soon as you feel up to it I'll walk you back to your cabin."

"No," She reached down deep within her and somehow found the strength to overcome the paralyzing fear that gripped her. "I came here to do a job and I will do it." Squaring her shoulders she drew a deep breath and got to her feet. With a determined look at Joe she asked, "Now what were you saying about a harness?"

Joe, with a glance at His brother-in-law, resumed filling her in on the procedure. Emma listened closely asking an occasional question, and by the time Jody arrived, she had regained her composure. Years of self-imposed control stood her in good stead as she schooled her features into a polite mask. She acted and reacted with all her emotions well in hand.

Sue noticed a subtle difference in Emma's manner as they prepared lunch. Though she was curious about what might have brought about the change, she decided against commenting on it.

Emma avoided Jake as much as possible during clean up. As they finished wiping the kitchen Jake, who had been watching her closely suggested that she rest for awhile before Gracie arrived. She thanked him and left without a backward glance.

Jake shook his head as he watched her go he made a mental note to sleep with his window open in case she had another nightmare.

Chapter 3

"Doctor Harold Linden's office."

"Hello Veronica, this is Emma Winters. Is Doc in?"

"Oh, hi Emma. The Doctor is expecting your call."

"I'll bet he is."

"Let me put you on hold for a moment," she said soothingly. "I'll tell him you're on the line." Veronica couldn't help grinning she had been Doc's receptionist for many years and had seen, first hand, some of the tactics he had used on the poor girl. She'd known a major storm was brewing, when Doc had told her with a chuckle, that when Emma called, not to keep her waiting. The phone lines might not be able to handle the strain.

"Emma how nice to hear from you. Are you all settled in?" Doc asked warily.

"Exactly what are you trying to pull?" Emma's voice shook with fury.

"Now Em-"

"Don't 'now Em' me," she sputtered. "You knew what kind of ranch this was. How can you be so heartless, so cruel, soo...?"

"So concerned, so loving, so desperate. Emma calm down and listen to me." Doc's voice was stern. "I'm glad you're furious, at least it's not that shallow farce of an emotion you put on most of the time. You can't possibly know how long I've prayed for an opportunity such as this, to come along."

"But, disabled kids?" Emma sputtered. "How could you?"

"Listen to me. It's high time you quit hiding from life. Things happen. Birth defects happen. They aren't always the fault of the parents and in Angel's case it certainly wasn't your fault at all."

"No in my case it was negligence that killed Angel!" She cried bitterly.

"No Emma, no! Angel was very fragile; she didn't survive the heart surgery because she was just too weak." Doc took a deep breath and continued. "I didn't tell you this before, but Angel's development was so stunted, that there was no chance she would live. Dr. Hanson is the finest neonatal surgeon in the country and he couldn't save her. He knew you were a bad candidate for the surgery, but I begged him to do it anyway, even though the tests showed it was unlikely the baby would survive. Even if we had operated earlier she still wouldn't have made it. Intrauterine surgery is tricky in the best of circumstances, but in Angels case it was nearly impossible, her heart was too small, and the defect too severe."

"But, you don't understand." Emma wailed plaintively. "I can't stay here. I can't face any child without wondering how Angel would have looked, or how she would have acted, or if she would have blamed me." She murmured, "Sometimes, I think God must be punishing me for not seeking medical attention earlier."

"Emma honey, God isn't punishing you for what happened. You are torturing yourself. God wants to take the pain and bitterness away from you and give you a new life in him."

"I can't...I, I just can't believe that he would do that for me. Don't you see? It's easier for me to just put it out of my mind and try to pretend it never happened."

Doc decided to take a different approach, his voice shook as he spoke gently. "Emma, Martha and I love you so much. We can't stand seeing you like this any more. You're not just our goddaughter. Since your parents died, you've been our pride and joy and we're praying for you daily. Please Em, won't you stay there? You need to discover that there are living, breathing, precious human beings out there disguised by disabilities. Children, who need you every bit as much, as you need them. Don't close your eyes and your heart to them. You are alive. Angel wouldn't want you to stop living. You need to face up to this Emma or you'll regret it for the rest of your life."

The silence on the other end of the phone stretched

on for what seemed an eternity, as Doc waited for her reply. Finally she spoke in a small voice, "I don't think I can."

"Honey, please. You are the strongest person I've ever known. There are women right now, in institutions and graveyards that were unable to live with what you've gone through. Five years, you've lost five years to pain. Don't let it ruin the rest of your life. I know you want to do this your own way, but after all this time you're more withdrawn than ever before. If you need someone to talk to you can call Martha or me, or go to Sue." Doc's voice was hoarse with passion and tears ran down his face as he pleaded. "Please Em, promise me you'll stay."

Emma knew she was fighting a losing battle. Doc had stood by her, and supported her through the darkest times of her life. She didn't want to stay, but how could she refuse his impassioned pleas?

"Alright, I'll stay," she whispered and the phone went dead.

Replacing the receiver, Doc breathed a prayer, "It's all in your hands now, Lord. Thy will be done."

*   *   *

What have I gotten myself into? Emma wondered as she set out for the corral. Why had she let Doc talk her into staying? He had to know how it tore her apart to see these children. At least, Angel hadn't appeared physically deformed, even though she had been premature. No! She shook her head, she wouldn't think about her. She would not dwell on the past. Firmly she closed the door on her memories.

"Fine, I'll do my job, but no more. I will not get involved."

"Now that's right hard to do Miss Emma." Ken the stable boss stood looking at her.

"I'm sorry; I didn't realize I spoke aloud." Moving to stand near the corral fence, she rested her arms on the top rail to try and control their shaking. "I don't usually do that."

Ken joined her and drawled thoughtfully. "You have a tough job cut out for you, if you think you can keep you're distance from them little fellers. They have a way about 'em. Just when you're sure you're okay one of 'em gets their arms around you're neck and they go right down to you're heart." Shaking his head he chuckled.

"I can handle it." Emma stiffened her back and marched into the barn. Into her heart indeed. What that dear old man didn't know was that Emma had no heart. It had stopped long ago and even though the doctors had restarted it, she refused to allow it to function in any capacity, other than pumping blood.

Gracie was already at the barn when Emma approached. Joe and Jake were deftly buckling on the harness that would keep her safe.

There was an impish quality about the child. From

her light brown ponytail and freckles to her red tennis shoes, Emma could easily see that she would be a handful.

"Who's that?" The girl pointed at Emma.

"Gracie, this is Miss Emma." Joe introduced her. "She's our new helper. Do you think you could show her how we do things here?"

The child examined Emma with wide brown eyes that seemed to see clear through her. Then with a solemn expression she introduced herself.

"I'm Gracie Callahan and I'm eight years old." Taking the job seriously, she launched into Emma's orientation. "When I was six, the Doctor had to cut off my leg 'cause I had cancer. See?" she pulled up the left leg of her jeans. Below her knee was the steel bar of a prosthetic leg. "My friend Casey has a leg that looks real, but I like this one. I can run faster, on account of it isn't as heavy," she wiggled her 'leg' in demonstration. "All the kids think it's cool."

The candid way she spoke about her disability surprised Emma, who would not even allow herself to think about such things.

The little girl didn't need much help, and once she was settled into the saddle, her "feet" firmly planted in the adjustable stirrups, Gracie asked. "Do you ride Miss Emma?"

"Yes, but I haven't ridden in quite some time."

"You should. Why don't you get a horse and we can go riding together."

Joe overrode the wheedling tone in her voice.

"Oh no you don't. You aren't going to get Miss Emma embroiled in some harebrained scheme."

"Come on Mr. Joe, you know I can handle a horse and this harness won't let me fall."

"That's just it Gracie." Joe explained seriously. "If something were to happen, you couldn't ditch out. Say, a rattlesnake spooked your horse and it was running for a cliff. There's no way you could unbuckle the harness and kick loose. If your horse lost its footing and rolled down a bluff you would be crushed. I can't take that kind of chance with your life." Flicking her ponytail he smiled to soften the disappointment.

"Well, why didn't you tell me all that before? Now I can practice not needing this dumb old harness. I'll get so good I won't need it at all, you'll see." Determination rang in her voice and she straitened her back.

Emma couldn't help smiling a little; she had no doubt in her mind that Gracie would be soon riding on her own. This child reminded her of herself at that age.

When Gracie had finished with her lesson and thanked Joe and Emma for their help, she turned and walked with a slight limp to the gate. Grasping

Jake's hand she asked in a loud whisper. "Do you think when I grow up, I'll be as pretty as Miss Emma?"

Jake smiled into Emma's startled eyes, "Why, yes ma'am, I think you will."

Embarrassed, Emma turned and fled into the barn to check that everything was in order. Children were so…open about everything. Angel would have been a lot like Gracie. The fleeting thought passed through her mind. What was wrong with her? She had worked for too long to keep these sort of thoughts bottled up. She was not going to let them out now. Sighing she turned to go.

Jake smiled as he entered the barn. "If you feel up to it, we can saddle up some horses and I'll show you around the ranch so you can get used to the feel of a horse again."

Emma considered his offer. Here was a man she felt she could trust. She was impressed with the fact that he hadn't taken advantage of the situation this morning when he was in her cabin, and she wasn't worried about being alone with him now. She had always loved horses and if she was going to be at the ranch, she might as well get used to being in the saddle again.

"Do we have the time before I need to start dinner?" She surprised him by asking.

"There's plenty of time. We won't go very far your first time out." Jake led the way to the far end of the stable. "Ken, Miss Emma and I are going to get Ginger and the Black ready ourselves."

Emma knew he was testing her to see how much she actually knew about horses, but she didn't mind. From the time she had been Gracie's age she had gone to camp every year, first as a camper, then for a year as a counselor until her parent's death. Horses had always been her favorite part of camp and she would have slept at the stables if they'd let her. Selecting the proper tack, she saddled Ginger under Jake's watchful eye and mounting their horses, they set off.

Taking the path along the river, Jake pointed out the trail that led to the swimming hole. They wound through the trees and turned onto a wide bridle path that encircled the ranch buildings. Wildflowers carpeted the ground and perfumed the air as they rode.

Jake was impressed with the way Emma handled Ginger; she had a gentle touch and moved gracefully in the saddle. She obviously knew what she was doing.

"There's no topping the Rocky Mountains in springtime." Jake smiled. "I've been a lot of places, but there's nowhere I've felt as comfortable as I do right now."

"It's beautiful here," Emma nodded. "I don't think I've ever seen a place with such a perfect view."

"If you like this, you should see the view from

Lookout Point. On a clear day, you can see for miles."

"Lookout Point? Is it near here?"

Jake pointed to a rocky outcropping atop a bluff rising to the north. "It's up there, it's not accessible by road, but one day we could take the horses up, if you'd like."

"Does that mean I've passed the riding test?" Emma glanced sideways at him.

"There's only one more thing I want to check. Let's see how you handle Ginger at a run." With a touch of his heels, he urged The Black into a canter.

Emma flew past him as they raced down the broad path. Wind tugged at her hair and tried to dislodge the straw cowboy hat she wore low over her forehead. Blood pounded through her veins, she urged her mount into a fast run as skimming along at breakneck speed she moved as one with the powerful animal.

Reaching a bend in the path, they pulled the horses to a reluctant stop. Ginger and the Black tossed their manes and snorted in noisy protest. Deftly controlling the excited animal, Emma, who gave every impression of wanting to continue the run as much as the horses surprised Jake with her first genuine laugh. The physical activity had brought a deep glow to her skin and her eyes were shining. No longer were they cold and gray, but sparkling blue green.

Jake was amazed, the transformation was remarkable and he felt something deep within him spring to life. In one brief moment, he saw something within her that few people had seen in years. Then abruptly, as if a door had closed, she was under control again, and the high wall that kept him from that wonderful person he'd seen was firmly back in place. He found himself wanting to scale the wall she had erected, and like knights of old, rescue the princess on the other side. Shaking his head at such absurd fantasies he prayed silently for guidance as they returned to the stable.

Ken met them on their return and reached for the reigns of Emma's horse. "Go on ahead Miss Emma. I'll take care of Ginger so's you can get supper goin'."

Emma checked her watch and slid to the ground.

"Thanks Ken, I really shouldn't let you take care of my mount for me, but I do need to get to the kitchen."

"Don't you worry about it one little bit. You can take care of her next time." Ken waved her away and led Ginger into the barn.

Jake followed with The Black, and cross tying the horses they removed the saddles. Ken handed Jake a brush and they got down to business.

"Thet girl sure could use some help." Ken observed quietly.

"Uh huh," Jake muttered.

"I thought we were goin' ta lose her fer a minute this mornin'."

"Uh huh."

"Doc's pretty cagey."

"Uh huh."

"There must be a special reason he sent her here."

"Uh huh."

"She sure is purty."

"Uh-hey! Are you trying to get me in trouble?" Jake grinned.

"Nope, I jest wanted to see if you was listenin'," Ken chuckled. "We got our work cut out for us with this one."

"I get the impression that she doesn't want our help."

"She wants our help," Ken grinned, as they turned the horses into their stalls. "She just doesn't know it yet, but at least she's still here. I was afeared she'd bolt and run this mornin'."

"Emma's strong, and she's stubborn." Jake shook his head. "I'm afraid that, that's a lethal combination."

"It's nothin' our Lord can't handle. Let's tell him

about it." Reverently removing their hats, they bowed their heads in prayer.

*   *   *

The days fell into a routine, for which Emma was thankful. Slowly, she began to unwind to the point where she felt comfortable around most of the staff, with the exception of Romeo. He had been polite, but there was still a flirtatious undercurrent whenever he was around and she tried to keep her distance from him, as much as possible. It helped that Joe kept him busy on the range checking on the cows and calves.

For the most part, the friendly atmosphere at the ranch was such that there wasn't a constant need to keep her guard up. As Ken had told her, it was nearly impossible to remain detached from the children. The more she tried to remind herself not to become too involved, the harder it became. Quite often she found herself smiling at some silly thing they said, and more than once she had been the recipient of wild hugs and sweet kisses.

Four-year-old Jody was fascinated by Emma's curls. He usually found a way to pull the ponytail holder from her hair. Emma had a hard time chastening him. He wasn't rough, and he never actually pulled her hair, he simply held onto it. He seemed to enjoy the texture, as he ran his small hands through the silky mass. She finally gave up trying to keep her hair back when he was around. He was a precocious child with a smile that did strange things to her heart every time she saw it.

"You need to be more firm with that boy," Joe shook his head as Emma tried unsuccessfully to corral her hair back into its customary ponytail after one such episode.

"It's not a matter of being firm." Emma explained carefully. "You'll notice that his mother's hair is seldom tidy. She told me that from the time Jody was a small baby, he always held onto her hair. He treats hair like a security blanket and whenever a child is stressed he'll reach for what will calm him."

Jake nodded, "I've noticed a similar situation with Brandon. He doesn't suck his thumb until he gets near a horse, then you can't get it out of his mouth."

"Well Em, as long as you don't mind looking like you've been mauled by a bear, I guess we'll just have to wait and see if he grows out of it," Joe grinned, as Ken came out of the stable

"Here you go Miss. Emma." Ken handed Emma a currycomb. "You seem to be havin' some trouble there."

"Very funny Ken," Emma crossed her arms and fixed him with a disapproving stare. "And here, I was going to offer you fellows a cup of coffee and some leftover cinnamon rolls from breakfast."

"Aw now, we was only jokin'. You know us well enough by now, to know we don't mean nothin' by it." Ken tried, but failed, to look repentant, as Jake and his brother-in-law pasted, what they hoped were engaging little boy grins on their faces.

Emma held her pose for as long as she could, but when Ken added his boyish grin and with a flourish, offered her his arm, she had to relent. Her lips twitched as she clapped her broad-brimmed hat on her head.

"Okay, come on. It's getting too hot out here to argue with you." she tucked her hand into the proffered arm and allowed Ken to lead her to the kitchen.

Sue looked up with a smile when they came through the door. "I thought you might take a break, so I made some coffee."

"Mmm, beauty and intelligence. What more could a man ask for?" Joe wrapped his arms around his wife and kissed her soundly.

"Some soap and water would do for starters." Sue teased as Joe headed for the sink.

Sue grinned as she watched Emma hang up her hat. "I see you had Jody this morning. I used to wear my hair in a braid to keep it from getting tangled."

"Finally, someone with some practical advise." Emma grinned ruefully as she ran her hands through her tangled tresses. "You guys could have told me that a week ago and spared me this trouble."

"And miss the scenery? I don't think so. Hey!" Joe jumped as Sue poked him in the ribs. "I'm not the only guy, who thinks so," he looked appealingly to the other men for back up.

"I'm not so sure I should bail you out on this one," Jake teased. "But, I can't deny the truth." His eyes twinkled as he gazed appreciatively at Emma's tousled curls. "I agree with Jody."

Emma blushed deeply and fled to the restroom amidst amused chuckles. She stepped to the mirror and stared at her reflection in amazement. Who was that wild-haired woman with flushed cheeks and sparkling eyes? She hadn't minded being teased by Joe and Ken, but Jake was a different story. It had been so long since she was able to trust any man, other than Doc, and she wasn't sure she wanted to start now. Of all the men she had known in her adult life, Jake was most likely to get under her guard. He was a good man and a good Christian and if he found out about her past…she would just have to be more careful. Where Jake was concerned, she needed to keep her defenses firmly in place.

Jake had been through deep pain and loss over the death of his family and Emma felt some kind of a connection with him. There was nothing she could pinpoint exactly, but the feeling was there, none the less. She was trying to keep him at arms length, but it was hard, considering she worked so closely with him. Instinctively, she knew that he would never physically harm her in any way. When she was near him she felt protected and safe, and yet, there was also a strong physical attraction that bordered on the ridiculous. Part of her wanted to run as far away as she could get from him, and the other part wanted to throw her into his arms and cling to him forever. What would it be like, to be loved by a man like Jake Peterson? Pure Heaven, she was sure. Unfortunately, she would never find out.

Oh, why couldn't she be normal? Why did she have to feel everything so acutely? Even as a child she had been sensitive. That was how she had ended up at the barn that first year at camp when she was eight years old. She had been teased about her freckles and mousy brown hair that reminded her so much of Gracie. Seeking solitude she'd headed for the stable, to hide and lick her wounds. Mac had found her there and given her a handkerchief to mop up her tears. He'd listened, with an occasional nod of his grizzled head, as she told him all her woes, allowing her to follow him around and help with the animals. By the time she had finished her tirade, she was no longer angry. Mac gently pointed out another side of the situation, explaining that many times people took their own fear and frustrations out on those around them. He'd helped her understand that those girls were probably just homesick and in need of a friend.

Emma saw Mac's gentle ways reflected in Ken. Years of dealing with fractious animals had given them insight in how to calm a fractious child.

If only it was as easy to heal a fractured heart.

Emma sighed and tried to smile pleasantly as she opened the door and went to join the others at the corner table.

"Emma, back me up here." Sue called, as Emma poured some coffee. "I think the men have been working too hard, they need a day off now and then."

"You know we can't let all the men off at the same time. I stagger their days off so we won't be short handed, and they have most of the day off on Sunday's for Church." Joe looked seriously at his wife. "You're just feeling antsy because you can't get around more. You only have one week to go until you get your cast off, then I'm sure you'll feel better."

"We could celebrate Sue getting her cast removed, with a dinner party." Emma suggested. "I'll make a special dinner, and the men could bring their dates."

"Let's have a party instead," Sue enthused. "You know how things are out here. If we spread the word, all our friends and neighbors will come."

Emma looked nervous. "Without some major help, I don't know if I can prepare enough food for a large party."

"No problem. You don't know our friends, everyone will pitch in and, in no time, and we'll have more food than you can shake a stick at." Sue quickly launched into details and before long they had come up with a workable plan.

Over the next few days, Emma checked recipes and

wrote up a schedule for the day of the party. She spent extra time making sure everything would be perfect for Sue. Several times over the course of the last week she had noticed Sue looking a little peaked and she was worried about her.

Last Sunday, when they'd stopped for lunch after Church at the Last Chance Café, Mrs. Malone commented on Sue's lack of appetite, confirming that Emma wasn't imagining the difference in her employer.

"I hope this helps her to feel better," Emma sighed as she made her way to her cabin. The increasing heat of the day made her think longingly of the cold, clear water of the swimming hole. Her afternoon was free and although she should probably spend the time preparing for the party, Emma opted instead, for a swim. Quickly, she changed into a black one-piece swimsuit and pulled on a long tie-dyed T-shirt that hung halfway to her knees. Then slipping her feet into sandals, she gathered up her sunscreen and towel, and made her way to the river.

Emma sighed; she was paying the price for pushing herself too hard this past month. Six days a week she cooked and helped with the children, and on Sundays she made breakfast before Church. Then, even though she had the rest of the day free, she spent the time either in the kitchen preparing for the coming week or in her cabin, working on her music. The job itself wasn't that difficult, but she hadn't been sleeping well. Just last night she had driven herself to a state of exhaustion, before collapsing into bed only to toss and turn with strange dreams. Even now, the memory stayed with her, weighing heavily on her mind and blotting out the beauty surrounding her.

Children with obvious disabilities ran and played through her dream as if they had no physical problems at all. They called to her and she tried to go to them, but her legs and arms wouldn't move. To her horror, she realized that she was the disabled one, paralyzed in a wheelchair and unable to ward off the danger she sensed nearby, lurking in the background. She tried to call out and warn them of the danger, but she couldn't speak. Gasping and crying, she'd struggled awake, wrapped in the bedclothes and bathed with cold sweat.

Emma tried to shake off the effects of the dream and concentrate on her surroundings. Every time she came down here, she was struck again by the beauty of the setting. A concrete dam had been placed at a bend in the shallow river. It had slowed and deepened the water, giving the swimming hole a small man made waterfall at the outlet. Sand had been hauled in, to make a white beach. Yellow pine, cottonwood and scrub oak trees lent an air of privacy to the lovely scene. The beauty of her surroundings washed over Emma like a balm, easing her tired spirit

Emma dropped her towel and T-shirt on the beach and was rubbing sunscreen on her shoulders when she realized she was not alone. Shading her eyes against the glare of sunlight on the water, Emma made out the figure of a man lying propped on one elbow, watching her from the swimming raft. Her heart beat a rapid tattoo as she reached for her things and turned to leave.

"Come on in, the waters fine." Jake called.

Emma's first instinct had been to turn tail and run, but she hesitated uncertainly, and called out, "I'm sorry, I didn't know anyone was down here. I don't want to disturb you."

"You won't bother me," Jake's friendly voice calmed her fears. "I was hoping someone would come along and keep me company."

Feeling self-conscious, Emma tentatively waded out into the cold water. "Are you going to subject me to more worn out clichés, if I stay?"

"I might. Some days I can be full of them."

Emma laughed in spite of herself. "How deep is the water at the raft?"

"This time of the year it's about ten feet. Can you swim?" Emma nodded. Jake followed her slow progress with a watchful eye. "You could use just swing out and drop from the rope. It's the quickest way to get in."

"Not now, I like to give myself a little more time to get used to the water, but it looks like fun." Emma eyed the thick rope, which was tied to a large, overhanging branch of an ancient cottonwood tree near the water.

"Later in the summer, when the water gets low, we quit diving from the raft and use the rope to jump in."

Emma had been easing into the frigid pond as they talked. The water was crystal clear and ice-cold. She waded until the water reached her waist, then bracing herself, she took a deep breath and dove in, swimming about fifteen feet underwater before surfacing with a gasp and striking out quickly for the raft.

"It takes a few minutes to get used to the water," Jake grinned as she climbed, shivering, up the ladder. "If you don't stay out too long, it won't be so hard to get back in."

"I came out here to get cooled off, and it worked." She rubbed her hands briskly up and down her arms as she sat on the edge of the float and dangled her feet in the water.

The air suddenly seemed to be charged with static electricity. The sensation made Jake unaccountably nervous. He glanced around desperately for something, anything to say that would ease the situation.

"Avoid the rocks on the other side of the pond; it's the kind of place rattlesnakes might hide."

"Snakes?" Emma pulled her feet up and looked askance at the rocks.

"I said, there may be some in the rocks, not the water, you silly goose." Jake chuckled; he was still slightly off balance and didn't stop to think how his comment would sound.

"Hey, I know better than to climb around on rocks. I grew up a few hours from here and I'm not totally stupid." Emma groused defensively, she disliked being made to feel foolish in front of him. "I also know that rattlers prefer a sunny rock to swimming in melted glacier water."

Jake held his hands up in a gesture of surrender. "I'm sorry, I wasn't thinking. I know you have enough sense to stay off the rocks. Truce?"

Emma eyed him thoughtfully then nodded her head. "Truce," she intoned solemnly. They sat quietly for a moment.

"How are the plans for the party going?"

"Fine, but I'm not sure we'll have enough food."

"Are you kidding? With five ranch hands and Ken, we have six eligible men between the ages of twenty and sixty on the place, not to mention a young unattached woman. Neighbors for miles around will come, bearing their own specialty dishes and checking out the competition."

"That's good news about the food, but don't add me to the list of available singles. I may be unattached, but I am not competition." She shot him an inquiring glance. "I noticed you didn't include yourself in the number of unattached males. Are you still grieving for your wife?"

Emma was shocked. Whatever possessed her to ask him such a question? It wasn't as if she was interested in him for herself. It must be that he was becoming such a good friend, that she didn't want him to get hurt any more than he already had been. It was strange, but she had the feeling that she would do anything to keep him from getting hurt. Well, almost anything.

"In some ways, I don't think you ever stop grieving for your loved ones, but that's not the reason I think of myself as unavailable. I'm just not interested in the whole dating ritual." Jake joined her at the edge of the raft and dropped his feet into the water next to hers.

"I know what you mean. When I worked in the clubs I saw people at their best and at their worst." She turned her head away and tried to keep the tension out of her voice, "It's not a scene I'm interested in either." Taking a deep breath she tried to smile.

Jake wanted to ask about her past, but he could tell she didn't want to talk about it. He opted instead for a change of subject.

"Sue mentioned that you work for a studio."

"Yes," she was always wary when people asked about her work, she could usually put them off with a few inane technical statements, but she was afraid that wouldn't work this time. Judging from the set up in her cabin, she was certain this man knew far more about recording than he was letting on.

"What do you work on?"

"Just a little this and that," she hedged. "What about you? I've noticed that you aren't exactly a ranch hand."

"You're right," he shrugged. "I guess you could say, I'm between careers at the moment. Joe and Sue have been kind enough to let me stay here until I decide what I want to do, and in return, I help out doing whatever's necessary."

"Well, if you decide to take up a career as a dishwasher I'd be happy to give you a good reference." Emma laughed.

"Thanks, I may need to take you up on that some day."

Emma knew there was a lot that Jake wasn't telling her. He didn't have the bearing of an out of work drifter. He was the type of man who would be comfortable doing just about anything, from washing dishes to presiding over the boardroom of a multi-million dollar corporation.

"Hold still and watch carefully." Jake pointed down into the water. "Can you see the fish?"

Emma scanned the water in the direction Jake was pointing. Beneath the surface she could make out the sleek forms of several fish. "I see them. What do you think they are?"

"Wal Ma'am," Jake drawled with an exaggerated accent. "I can't be real sure, but I'd say they look ta be fish."

"Why, my heavens, kind Sir." Emma surprised them both by picking up the accent and playing along. She even went so far as to bat her eyelashes at him. "I truly meant to inquire as to the kind of fish they might be?" Then she burst out laughing at the expression of unbelief on his face.

Jake swallowed hard on the excitement he felt rising within him. This was the first playful thing he had seen her do, that didn't involve the children. In that instant, a bond as fragile as a silken thread, tentatively wound itself around their hearts. Pulling them together as only laughter can do.

"Brook Trout," he smiled widely, as he eyed her swimsuit. "You wouldn't happen to have a fishing pole in your pocket, would you?"

"Not today," she laughed. "I didn't wear the swimsuit with pockets."

"Do you like to fish?"

"I used to, but I'm afraid I was never any good at it."

"I'm not surprised." He teased. "I'll bet you were one of those kids, who wouldn't hold still long enough to drown a worm."

"There was way too much to do, and too many places for me to explore." She threw him an inquiring glance. "How did you know?"

"Because I haven't seen you hold completely still since you moved here and, you haven't been still since you sat down either. Do I make you nervous?" Jake smiled into her startled eyes.

"No, I'm more comfortable with you than with anyone I know." Emma dropped her gaze. To her horror she could feel a blush creeping into her cheeks. She wasn't sure what had gotten in to her. For a while there she had almost felt, well... normal.

"Thanks, I'll take that as a compliment." They sat for a few minutes in companionable silence.

"See the mountain peaks through break through the trees?" Jake pointed. Have you ever seen such breathtaking scenery as we have here in Colorado?"

"I spent the summer after High School traveling through Europe with friends. There was some incredible scenery, but it just made me homesick for the Rocky Mountains."

"Did you back pack through Europe?"

"Hardly. Doc never would have allowed such reckless behavior. After my parents died Doc and Martha became my guardians. They let me go on an organized tour with my friends Mandy and Beth, we were well chaperoned."

"I'll bet you tried to sneak out."

"We didn't actually need to," she chuckled. "We were too busy trying to keep the chaperone in line."

Jake burst out laughing, his face alive with merriment. Emma watched him from under her thick fringe of lashes enjoying the way his eyes crinkled at the corners when he smiled. She had seen a myriad of thoughts and emotions in his eyes. Most days they were like an open book, filled with laughter, concern, intelligence and such peace that she longed for what she saw in them. Once, in an unguarded moment, she saw loneliness and remembered pain. Even now she wanted to keep the smile in those wonderful eyes. If she could, she would reach out and wipe away all his hurtful memories, leaving only the good behind.

For one revealing moment her guard came down and all the pain, bitterness and longing poured into her face. It wasn't until Jake covered her hand with his that she realized she was lost in the velvet depths of his gaze. Hot color flooded her face as she dropped her eyes and turned away. She took a deep breath and tried to disengage her hand.

"Emma please, don't pull away." Jake turned her towards him "What's wrong."

"Nothing's wrong," she bluffed.

"You can't fool me. Something's wrong."

"Look, I just don't want to talk about it."

"Okay, I'll drop it for now, but if you ever need someone to talk to, I'm here. That's what friends are for." He squeezed her hand before releasing it

"Thanks," she swallowed hard and smiled slightly, her defenses firmly back in place. She needed to change the subject before he pushed the issue any further and she wound up telling him everything. "That water is really gong to be cold now, and we can't ease in slowly this time."

"Sometimes it's better to plunge right in and get it over with all at once." The double meaning of his words wasn't lost on her.

"That's easy for you to say, but I don't see you in a hurry to dive into ice water." Emma resorted to humor to clear the air. "Come on, a friend wouldn't let me do this alone," she grinned sweetly.

Her ability to swiftly change conversational gears was sometimes a little disconcerting, but it was the teasing light in her eyes that Jake found irresistible. Rising to his feet he challenged, "I'll race you to the dam. That is, if you can stand the cold."

"You're on," she joined him at the edge of the raft.

"Okay, on the count of three," Jake joined her. "One, two, three!" They were off.

The shock of cold water was soon forgotten in the exhilaration of exercise as their heads broke the surface of the crystal clear water. Jake was swimming easily beside her, and she suspected that he was deliberately holding back. They raced side by side until, with a sudden burst of speed, Jake pulled slightly ahead of her and reached the dam with a one-stroke lead.

Emma caught her breath and laughed. "Now I know why you need to change careers."

"Why?"

"You must be a former Olympic swimmer," she grinned.

"Aw, you found me out," Jake teased as he slapped the surface of the water and sent a cascade of droplets showering over her.

"Now you've going to get it, Mister." Emma grinned as she sent a sheet of water his way.

They splashed and swam like children until Emma gasped; "Oh my goodness what time is it? I need to start dinner."

Jake checked his waterproof watch. "You have plenty of time, but we'd better get going. You have a good tan, but your nose is starting to get pink."

Emma resisted the urge to look cross-eyed at her nose while they waded to shore. Jake retrieved his things from the stump where he had left them, and quickly toweling off, they donned their T-shirts and sandals and headed up the trail.

"What are you making for dinner?" Jake asked.

"Spaghetti. Why, are you hungry?"

"I'm starved. What do you say to making a raid on the cookie jar?"

"And ruin your chances of an Olympic gold medal?" Emma laughed. "How about a meatloaf sandwich?"

"As long as it comes with cookies, don't forget that I'm no longer in the running for the Olympics."

Entering the kitchen, they surprised Slim with his hand literally in the cookie jar. His guilty expression was comical to say the least, and Emma was hard pressed not to laugh.

"Ah ha!" she scolded with pretended outrage. "That's where all my cookies have been going."

"Aw, Miss Emma, I'm still a growing boy, I gotta have something to eat and yore cookies sure do a fine job of fillin' an empty spot on a hot afternoon." Slim pleaded.

"Okay," Emma smiled. "How about a sandwich to go with them?"

"Uh, that's what I thought you'd say." Slim brought his hand from behind his back as he edged toward the door. "By the way, that sure was good meatloaf last night." He waved a thick sandwich at them as he disappeared through the door.

"Well, how do you like that?" Jake laughed. "I suppose this means I don't get a meatloaf sandwich."

"Now I know where the leftovers have been disappearing to. Emma explored the walk in cooler. "How about a chicken sandwich instead?"

"I could eat anything about now."

"I think I might have some anchovies around here somewhere."

Jake raised an eyebrow at her. "And you used to be such a nice quiet little thing. What's gotten into you?"

"I'm afraid to find out. Hand me a couple of plates, Mr. Olympic swimmer."

"Is this the spaghetti sauce?" Jake asked, passing her the plates and motioning to an industrial sized slow cooker.

"Yes, it's an old family recipe I let it simmer all day."

"No wonder you went swimming." Jake commented as he lifted the lid and sniffed appreciatively.

"What does spaghetti sauce have to do with swimming?" Emma threw him a confused glance.

"You couldn't stay in the same room with something that smelled like this and not want to eat every bite."

"Here's a spoon for a sample." Emma laughed at his

nonsense. "I'm almost finished with the sandwiches.

Jake tested the sauce and pronounced it perfect, while she set their filled plates on the corner table and poured them tall glasses of iced tea.

At Emma's request, Jake prayed over their food, and all was quiet for a few minutes as they attacked their snack.

Jake covertly watched Emma as they ate. Rays of sun peeked through the curtains beside her, burnishing her already, honey blonde curls and bringing a warm glow to her skin. At a glance she appeared to be just a normal light-hearted young woman, but the tension around her eyes and the dark smudges beneath them, attested to how tightly her nerves were stretched.

Earlier today, he'd had the privilege to witness a rare unguarded moment. The immeasurable pain he had seen in her eyes reminded him of the torment he had been through and proved to him that his earlier impressions were correct. Emotionally, Emma seemed to be poised, teetering on the edge of a deep precipice. Once again his protective instincts took over, and he prayed that he would be there to catch her when she fell.

"A penny for your thoughts."

The sound of her voice brought his mind up sharply, and Jake realized that he had been staring at her.

"I'm sorry, my mind was a thousand miles away."

"You looked so serious that you had me worried for a moment. Do you want to talk about it? That's what friends are for."

Jake grinned as he recognized the same phrase he had used on her; he chose his next words carefully. "I'm worried about a friend of mine. She's having problems, but she won't except my help. It seems like no matter what I do I can't get past her defenses." He mentally kicked himself for causing the friendly light to fade from her eyes.

"Your friend might not want your help. There are some things better off left alone. If you start poking around under rocks, you're likely to find a scorpion." Emma picked up their plates and turning to go she paused, and seemed to do battle with an unseen force. With her gaze averted she said, "I don't know about your friend, but I think you should give her some space. If she wants your help, she'll come looking for you."

"Fair enough." He rose to help with the clean up. He would be patient and bide his time.

Emma didn't know it, but wasn't ready to give up on her yet.

Chapter 4

"Were heading into town after lunch to have Sue's cast removed Joe waved a hand at his wife amidst cheers and congratulations.

Sue beamed. "I won't be able to get around real well yet, but I'll enjoy wearing two shoes for a change. I hope you all have a date lined up for the party tomorrow."

Emma smiled as she watched Joe and Sue. During the five weeks she had been at the ranch she had seen time and again, how much they meant to each other. Joe never failed to show his wife the respect and tenderness she deserved, even when he was teasing her unmercifully. Sue did likewise with a deep appreciation for her husband.

"We'll only work half a day tomorrow, so you'll have time to get ready and pick up your dates. You are, of course, expected to help with the preparations. Most will be done right after lunch. With everyone pitching in, it won't take very long." The men groaned good-naturedly and teased Joe about taking the afternoon off to go into the city. The mood was high as Joe finished giving the men their assignments for the day.

After the dishes were finished Emma headed out to work.

"We have a new client this morning, her name is Katie and she's three years old. She's new to large animals so we will have to take it slow so we don't frighten her. She had a heart condition as an infant. The problem was corrected, but she's still a bit frail." Joe informed them as a car drove in and parked at the main entrance. "Emma, would you mind picking up some cookies? I forgot to grab some when I left the kitchen."

"You're entitled to be a little forgetful occasionally." Emma headed for the short cut behind the stable. "I'll be right back."

Joe loved spoiling the kids. He reminded her in many ways of Doc. There were always treats for the children. Suckers, cookies, or stickers whichever the disability would allow. Smiling to herself she went to retrieve the sugar cookies she kept hidden from sight in a large canister. If Slim found them there would be none for the kids.

The kitchen was filled with food for the party. Emma skirted cases of chips and buns left on pallets by the door. Thank heavens Slim and Bert, one of the other men, had already stacked the cases of meat and soft drinks in the walk in cooler. Joe and Sue had helped with the ordering and organizing of the supplies. Without their help it would have been a nightmare.

Thinking about nightmares reminded her of the first

time she had seen Jake, she remembered again, the warmth in his eyes and the safety of his arms. She rubbed her arms to dispel the goose bumps, which rose despite the mid-morning heat.

Returning with the treats she met Katie. She was very taken with the child. From the top of her blonde curly head to her slightly thin legs, she was a bundle of talkative energy.

When they placed her on a small placid pony she squealed and clung to Emma. Without thinking Emma quietly began to sing. She had done it before when she thought no one was in hearing distance, but this time Jake was on the other side of the pony. After a surprised glance, he grinned and joined her.

Emma wrote the song 'Daddy's Girl' while pregnant with Angel. It was a sweet song about the bond between a father and his little girl. She had avoided it like the plague for years and wasn't sure why it came so naturally to her lips now, but when Jake joined his voice to hers, the missing piece of the puzzle fell into place. Now she knew why he'd always sounded so familiar. His voice had been in her head numerous times and on the radio more times than she could count.

Jake Peterson was John Tabor the Country Music artist who'd recorded 'Daddy's Girl', and many other songs she had written. By the time they finished the first verse Katie was all smiles. She happily hugged everyone in sight and proclaimed them all her new 'bestest friends'.

Katie's visit ran a little long and Emma had to leave to start lunch so she praised the little girl and headed for the main building.

Humming softly, she walked into the kitchen and found Sue at the corner table drinking coffee with a pretty blonde.

"Here's Emma now, they must be about done with Katie's lesson. Emma this is Cindy Robertson, Katie's mom." It wasn't unusual for Sue to entertain parents, while their children had therapy. But, as the woman turned and Emma caught sight of her, she suddenly felt as though someone hit her hard, knocking the wind out of her.

Thankfully, Cindy misinterpreted the stunned look on Emma's face. "Emma, how are you? I haven't seen you since high school."

"I'm fine thanks," Emma smiled mechanically as she struggled for composure. "How are you?"

"I'm doing much better now that Katie is over with her last bout of the flu. I've been telling Sue that my little girl was born with a congenital heart defect. Dr. Hanson was able to correct the problem by surgery while she was still in the womb."

"It's incredible what they can do now," Sue piped in. She tried to draw Cindy's attention from her friends pale face, as Emma turned and began getting things together for lunch.

"It was a miracle that the Doctor discovered the

problem. I wasn't scheduled for an ultrasound that day, but it's a good thing they did one anyway." Cindy turned to Emma. "So how are you Em? Did you ever do anything with your singing career?" asked Cindy. As Emma shook her head she went on. "You should have heard her Sue, she was very good. She used to sing in clubs around town."

"That was a long time ago." Emma stated flatly.

Sue had never seen Emma so wooden before sensing the desperation in her friend; she gathered her crutches and suggested to Cindy that they go collect Katie.

"Bye Em, see you soon." Cindy called as she followed Sue out of the kitchen.

"It was nice seeing you again." Emma murmured automatically.

Moving around the kitchen on automatic pilot, Emma remembered the last time she had seen Cindy. It had been over a year after she had lost Angel. She was at a small restaurant downtown, trying to force herself to eat some lunch. She had just received her food when two women came in and took the booth behind her. Emma stared blankly at their reflection in a large mirror, barely registering that she had gone to High School with the brunette facing her. The other woman, a blonde had her back to Emma and she didn't recognize her voice. They had apparently been shopping for baby clothes. Emma lost her appetite as they enthused over each tiny item. Gathering her things to leave, she was riveted to her seat by the mention of Carl's name.

"I never expected Carl Robertson to settle down to a wife and kids." Enthused the brunette.

"I'm so happy," her companion sighed. "I have a handsome husband and a baby on the way. My life couldn't be more perfect. Carl keeps singing that song 'Daddy's Girl'. He say's he doesn't care if the baby's a boy or a girl as long as it's healthy. Isn't that the sweetest thing you've ever heard?"

A knife twisted in Emma's heart. Nausea rose up within her as she blindly left some bills on the table, and with her head averted, hurried out the door. Walking down the side of the building toward her car, morbid curiosity caused her to glance in the window to see the woman who was now Carl's wife. It was Cindy Bradford. Emma was shocked. Cindy was such a nice girl and even though they hadn't been close friends in high school, they now shared a terrifying bond.

Emma knew that Cindy's baby was in danger of having the same birth defect that Angel had died from, but she didn't know what to do about it. She couldn't just walk up and introduce herself as the woman Carl had…

Torturing herself, she remembered that Doc had told her it would only be fair to warn Angel's father about the defect, but she'd wanted no part of him. She knew what she had to do, but she wasn't quite sure how to do it. Finally, out of desperation, she called Doc. He knew at once there was something wrong.

"Doc, this is Emma."

"What's wrong, Honey/"

"I need your help."

"You know I'll do anything I can for you," He could hear her ragged breathing through the phone. "Emma, what's wrong?"

"I-Is Cindy Brad- uh, Cindy Robertson one of your patients?"

"Yes she is."

"I-I need you to-to test her baby for heart defects."

The words tore at Doc's heart. He knew how hard it must have been for her to speak them. "Sure honey, I'll have Veronica call her right away." The phone went dead.

Doc repeatedly tried to call her until late in the evening, but he got no response. Emma wanted to be alone in her torment.

The next day when he called, Emma answered the phone. Cindy's case was being transferred to Dr. Hanson. A few months later, Doc had let her know that the defect had been repaired. Later she had heard that the baby, a girl, had been born safely. The Robertson's had moved to Boston to be closer to the specialist that was monitoring her case. Never knowing that Emma had alerted Doc to the possible problem.

Now it seemed that they had been brought together again. Somehow it didn't seem quite fair that her past was being thrust upon her again. She was finally beginning to make friends and there was a real possibility she could have an almost normal life here. She held no ill feelings toward Cindy or Katie. Both were oblivious to Emma's connection in their lives, and she was desperate to keep it that way. If Cindy were to find out what happened so long ago, it would only bring her pain. Emma was glad Katie had been given the chance to enjoy life. It was more than Angel had been given.

No, she knew that wasn't right. Doc had made certain that she and Angel had the best medical care possible. Even as Dr. Hanson had done his best to bring a spark of life back into Angel's tiny body, she had heard Doc in the background praying.

Emma rubbed her hands wearily over her burning eyes. No more tears. All the tears in the world wouldn't change what had happened. Would she ever be free of the guilt that weighed so heavily upon her heart?

When Sue returned, Emma was at the sink busily washing lettuce.

"Cindy seemed nice, and that Katie, what a cutie! I hope to have a little girl who is that sweet, some day." Sue smiled longingly.

"Your children will be even more wonderful," Emma said in an even tone.

"Thanks." Sue sighed, and then asked curiously. "What was all that about you having a singing career?"

"That was a long time ago."

"Why did you quit?"

Emma stiffened, "Personal reasons."

"You must have been good. Cindy sang your praises all the way to the corral."

Irritation crept into Emma's voice. "Look, I'd really don't want to talk about it."

"Oh, Em I'm sorry," Sue rushed to apologize. "It's none of my business. Mom always said I was too nosy for my own good. Can you ever forgive me?"

"Of course I forgive you." Emma softened slightly. "I didn't mean to snap at you, I just don't like to talk about it."

"I understand, but if you ever need someone to unload on, I have spare shoulder." Sue smiled and patted her shoulder invitingly.

"You never can tell," Emma smiled back. "I may take you up on your offer, some time." For the second time that day she felt close to tears.

Joe and Sue left for Denver as soon as they finished

lunch, and Emma, who was putting the last of the pots and pans away, was looking forward to a little peace and quiet. Everything was ready for the party, and the music in her head had quieted since last night. She was contemplating a solitary visit to the swimming hole, when Jake suggested a horseback ride into the hills.

"I'm heading up to Lookout Point, if you're interested. The view from up there is incredible."

"I'd like that," her eyes lit up. "I could pack a snack and be at the stables in fifteen minutes."

"Will you bring cookies?"

"You and your cookies. Is peanut butter okay?"

"If it's in cookies," Jake grinned as he left to get the horses ready,

Emma hurriedly packed some fruit, cookies and bottled water. Then she stepped into the restroom before leaving.

Reaching for her hairbrush, she caught a glimpse of her reflection in the mirror. She was still too thin, but the sun had brought a healthy glow to her skin and hair. If it wasn't for the ever-present smudges beneath her eyes, she might be considered attractive.

Where did that come from, she wondered. Warm color flooded her cheeks as she quickly pulled her hair back into its severe ponytail. The last thing she was interested in was trying to attract a man.

So why did the image of a dark haired, dark eyed man with a voice like rich chocolate and a smile that could charm the birds from the trees, came swiftly to mind? Emma put a lid on the memory of publicity shots she had seen of John Tabor. Jake was a completely different man since he lost his family and she couldn't reconcile the John of old with the man she now knew. At any rate, she wasn't going to worry about it today. She was spending the afternoon with a friend, not a Country Music star. It wasn't like she was interested in him as a man. She would just put it out of her mind; she'd already had enough heartache for one day and she was determined to enjoy her afternoon off, if it killed her. Scooping up her hat, she made a face in the mirror and headed out the door.

Emma was still smiling as she entered the stable. Ken peered at her over the back of Ginger and commented that if horseback riding made her that happy, she should ride more often. Then, he had the audacity to grin at her pink cheeks.

Leaving the ranch buildings behind, Emma's mount fell in behind Jake, as he led the way along a path that wound slowly upwards. The path was narrow and conversation was kept at a minimum.

Emma knew she had been tense, but this whole business with Cindy had left her even more wound up than usual. She concentrated on breathing in the warm pine scented air. The gentle swaying motion of her horse was soothing and slowly, she began to feel the tension of the past weeks ease from her body.

As they climbed she started catching glimpses of the view between the trees. After a while the trail left the bluffs and wound through thick forest. It was cool and quiet under the canopy of trees. Pine needles, so thick they muffled the sound of the horse's hooves, covered the ground. Light filtered through the thick canopy of trees, giving everything a slightly greenish glow. Bright shafts of sunlight shone here and there lending an ethereal atmosphere to the day. A hush had settled over everything and Emma began to feel as if God himself must dwell here. She remembered the song she had worked on last night. The lovely melody drifted through her mind accompanied by words that were as far removed from her situation as the earth is from the stars.

I'm so glad you saved my soul, and came to make my spirit whole!

The peace I've sought has been restored, and now, my Lord, with you I'll soar!

It was nice sentiment, and perhaps for someone who hadn't been through the same things she had, it might even be true. All she knew was that it left her feeling dissatisfied and aware that she wanted more from her life than a mere existence.

Emerging into bright sunlight it took Emma a moment to focus on the vista opening before them. To the west, foothills fell away to gently rolling plains. In the distance a mountain range lifted it's face to the brilliant cobalt blue sky, dotted with fluffy white clouds. From where they were standing, they could turn around and see ridge, after dark forested ridge leading up to jagged snow-covered peaks. It was breathtaking.

Emma dismounted from her horse and stood in awe. Jake stood by her side and it seemed fitting for him to hold her hand. For an eternity they stood there drinking in the tranquility and beauty around them. "It makes me feel so small," she said in the barest of whispers. The vista before her, encouraged her to open herself up to the beauty surrounding her.

"I like to come up here and pray. I feel so close to God up here, like my own troubles are nothing. It helps me keep them in perspective." Jake smiled and motioned out across the plains. "Can you imagine what it must have been like to cross there in a covered wagon?" He asked as they sat down leaning against a fallen log.

"Those early pioneers amaze me. I can't begin to understand the difficulties they must have faced. It was such a vast undertaking." He fell silent lost in reflection. After a while he turned and looked at Emma. "You know," he observed thoughtfully. "I see that same pioneering spirit in you."

"Me?" Emma's eyes met his in surprise.

"Yes you. You have determination, an iron will, so to speak, that won't allow you to admit defeat." He looked at her with admiration.

"I think you call it 'stubbornness'." Emma colored and averted her eyes. She didn't want his admiration. "I can't let things get me down."

"Don't forget, I've seen the brick wall you put up whenever someone gets too close," he smiled.

"So, who is this 'friend' you told me about who puts up walls?" She asked hoping to steer the conversation away from herself.

"You caught me," he grinned. "You're the wall builder. I have to confess that I've been trying to build a ladder so I can get to know the person hiding on the other side."

"Oh, no you don't, there's a 'No Trespassing' sign." Shaking her head sadly she continued. "Besides, I'm afraid you may not like what you find. Some things are better left hidden"

"Not always. If you leave something buried long enough, it has a tendency to grow in our own eyes; it may not be as bad as you think."

Biting her bottom lip, she shrugged, looking out across the vista before them and feeling smaller than ever before. "Hiding behind walls has been the only way I've been able to survive until now, but I-I just don't know anymore. When I'm up here it all seems so, pointless," she sighed heavily. "I wish... some day maybe... I'd like to tear them down, one brick at a time."

"If you need someone to pass bricks to, I'd be glad

to help."

"Thanks."

They sat in companionable silence for a while, leaning back against the log. The sun was warm on the crown of their hats and after a few moments, Emma's eyes were drawn to Jake. Quietly, she studied his profile. He appeared to have gone to sleep, his eyes were closed and a thick fringe of lashes lay across his tanned cheeks. A strong nose and chin framed his full mouth that, even though he was now relaxed, she knew those lips could smile without warning bringing sunshine into an otherwise dreary day. Dark hair that was usually kept short curled rebelliously from under the brim of his Stetson. Her first opinion of him as a mountain of a man rang true. At six foot three with broad shoulders, he made her feel petite, and that was something very few people had been able to accomplish. How could he be so relaxed, while she always felt as nervous as a cat on a hot tin roof?

Emma thought about the loss of his wife and child. Loss was something she understood all too well. In some obscure ways, their past was similar, and in so many ways, completely different. How was he able to put the pain aside and continue living? There was a special quality in him, an assurance that no matter what happened he could handle it.

The other day at the swimming hole, he'd said he was between careers. Emma could understand if he didn't want to continue singing. There had been many times when she wanted to give up songwriting, but the music just wouldn't go away. She sighed, and shook her head.

"Want to talk about it?" he surprised her out of her reverie.

"I thought you were asleep."

"Nope." He pushed the brim of his hat up an inch. "What's on your mind?"

"I know who you are." She blurted out. "You're John Tabor. I recognized your voice when you sang to Katie, but don't worry. I respect your privacy. Your secret's safe with me."

"Well, now that you know about it," he sat up straighter and grinned. "Everyone at the ranch is in on my secret,"

Emma looked up at him, maybe it was the common bond of the music industry that brought this feeling of closeness, or maybe it was the warm light in his eyes that invited confidences. Whatever the reason, she felt as if she could ask anything of him. That he would understand and not try to psychoanalyze her as the counselors, Doc had forced on her, had tried to.

"Did you stop singing because of your wife and daughter?" It was a serious question and he answered in kind.

"That was the reason at first. You see, 'Daddy's Girl' came out not long after Candy was born, and the timing of it couldn't have been more perfect, it was my tribute to having a daughter. Her full name was Candace Marie Peterson, but we called her Candy. My mother's name was Marie and I wanted Candy to have something special from her grandmother. Amy and I were so happy." His voice grew thick with remembered pain as he turned unseeing eyes ahead of him.

"Then I lost them both in a car accident when Candy was three. I was in shock at first, and refused to acknowledge that they were really gone. I kept waiting for Amy to come walking through the door and say that there had been a terrible mistake, and they were all right. Then the reality of their deaths hit me one day while I was driving."

Emma knew how he had felt. Memories of those first months following Angel's birth and death sent a piercing pain through her. She wrapped her arms around her knees and hugged them tightly to her. The tears that she had denied herself earlier in the day now silently coursed down her cheeks, but she couldn't turn away.

"'Daddy's girl' started playing on the radio, and I realized that I would never be able to cheer Candy on to win a swimming trophy, or see her wear her prom dress, or walk her down the isle at her wedding, and that's when I broke down. I pulled the truck over and right there on the side of the road, I finally quit blaming God for what happened, and I gave my heart to Him. He filled me with so much love that there was no room left for guilt and remorse, it was gone."

The fact that he would share such a private memory with her had a profound effect on Emma. There was no doubt that what he was saying was the absolute truth, and she wanted what he had with all her heart.

Jake drew a deep breath and continued in a low voice. "I still miss my family, but Amy was a Christian and I know that she and Candy are in heaven waiting for me. I know without a doubt that some day I'll see them again."

Feeling her acceptance of his words, he turned his head and saw the deep hunger within her tear filled eyes. He stretched his hand out to her and looking into her eyes he continued. "Emma, I don't know anything about your past or what has happened to hurt you so, but I do know that Jesus can make you whole. Won't you give him all the pain, and bitterness like I did? If you receive Him, He'll make you a new creature too."

Emma closed her eyes and briefly thought over her life. Her parents had been Christians and she had gone to church most of her life, but she had quit going after the incident with Carl, because she felt unworthy to be in the presence of God. Then after she had lost Angel, she felt that God had turned his back on her, and in her bitterness she refused to turn to him for solace. Now she realized that God had been there all along, waiting for her to acknowledge him. She looked at the hand that Jake held out to her, and slowly, she reached out her hand and placed it in his.

"Please," she asked, "tell me how."

Praying together was one of the most natural things she had ever done, as one by one he helped her take down the bricks of the wall that separated her from forgiveness.

Chapter 5

The preparations were ready for the party and Emma hurried to her cabin to change. She smiled as she remembered Joe and Sue's reaction to her news last night. Emma had supper almost ready when they came in the door. Sue was still using the crutches for support and had a brace on her ankle but she was cast free.

Emma gave her a big hug and exclaimed over how thin her leg looked.

"Thin and hairy," Sue laughed surprised at the warmth she had felt in the gesture.

They visited while Emma put the finishing touches on supper. When she could no longer keep it in, she'd divulged her secret to Sue.

With tears in her eyes Sue's arms had, once again, gone around Emma's slight frame. "I'm so happy for you. We've been praying for so long," she'd breathed. "I wondered what happened. You're all lit up like a Christmas tree."

They were still laughing when the men came in for supper. The happy excitement in the air had been infectious.

That night Emma had slept like a baby and awoke to the day fresh and happy, with a prayer on her heart and a song on her lips.

After a quick shower, she used the blow dryer and styled her hair. Looking in the mirror, Emma was more than pleased with her efforts. The rhinestones in her headband rivaled the stars in her eyes as she allowed her hair flow loose in a riot of curls. The bloom in her cheeks had nothing to do with the small amount of make-up she had carefully applied.

Stepping into her dress she enjoyed the way the royal blue satin set off her tan and brightened the color of her eyes from dull gray to a sparkling deep blue. The bodice was sleeveless with a scoop neckline that fit her slim form well without clinging. The cloth flowed softly over her hips and flared out from her knees ending with a swish at her ankles. Her delicate thin strapped sandals were low heeled and should be comfortable enough.

Twirling around, she caught her reflection in the full-length mirror. The whole effect brought a smile to her face. Catching up her matching shawl she headed for the kitchen to check on her hors d'oeuvres.

Jake was just leaving his cabin as she approached. He stood stock still, with a stunned look of shock on his face, as a vision of loveliness stopped before him. The setting sun behind her gave the illusion of a fiery halo around her head, and she wore a radiant smile on her delicate face. For a moment he just stared. Then his smile matched hers as he fell into step beside her.

"I'm afraid we may need sunglasses tonight."

"Excuse me?"

"Once the boys see your thousand watt smile they'll all be blinded," he teased.

"I'll try to tone it down," she laughed delightedly. "But, oh Jake, I'm just so happy."

He could tell. She fairly vibrated with happiness and his heart sang with her.

Once in the kitchen she wrapped a voluminous apron around her and Jake found himself wishing she would wear it all night.

Soon the guests began arriving. Neighbors and friends poured in, and Emma had a hard time keeping names and faces straight. Jake had been right; every guest came bearing at least one dish of food and Emma had more help than she ever dreamed possible.

Tonight the dining room shone. Candles in the center of each table gave off a soft glow. The double doors leading to the terrace were open and strings of colored lights softly, illuminated the scene. Patio torches burned here and there adding a festive light to the gathering darkness.

The fireplace in the great room was burning and candles in cut glass holders continued the welcoming atmosphere. Here also the French doors were opened and a soft breeze wafted through keeping the room from becoming stuffy.

The men were flattering with their praise and Emma took special pains to be friendly to their dates. Recorded music began playing and many couples turned to the dance floor.

Glad for the break Emma headed for the kitchen checking the buffet table as she went. Everything was tidy and she thanked the women keeping a close eye on things for her. She had been touched by the way that the kindly neighbors had jumped in to help, shooing her out of the kitchen.

Emerging from the kitchen she found herself face to face with her godparents.

"Emma?" There was a question in Doc's voice as he stared at her glowing face. The answer lay in the freedom he saw deep in her eyes. "Thank God." He breathed as he tenderly enfolded her in his arms. He wiped his eyes as Martha took her turn exclaiming over her transformation.

Disengaging herself, Emma led the way to a quiet corner where she happily answered all of their when's and how's.

"It's incredible, we've been waiting and praying for this for years," Doc smiled.

"Did you have this in mind when you talked me into taking this job?" Emma smiled fondly at her guardian.

"I've been praying for the right opportunity for you to see the love of God in action for as long as I can remember." Doc's kindly blue eyes misted over with emotion.

"I felt it was time for you to understand that life does go on after tragedy. Each person at the ranch has their own story of how God has brought them through pain and adversity. The stories aren't mine to tell, but if you'll look closely enough you can see how God has used their troubles to enrich their lives."

"Like Jake?" Emma asked.

"Yes. Exactly like Jake, he's already been through a lot and he still has a long way to go before he gets back on track. I think you might help him get back in the saddle."

"You mean with his music?"

"Among other things. How did you find out?"

"His voice was familiar, but when I heard him sing for one of the children yesterday it finally dawned on me who he was." She looked at him speculatively. "Did you send me here because you knew he was here?"

"No, but I was happy to learn he was still here. Does he know who you are yet?"

"Not yet, but you know, I don't think I'd mind him

knowing. He's the kind of friend who can keep quiet about important things."

"Emma dear," Martha smiled. "You don't know how happy it makes me to hear you refer to someone as a friend. You've been alone for such a long time and, believe it or not, you're going to need all the friends you can get."

Emma nodded, "I know there will still be hard times, and being a Christian doesn't make me perfect or take away my past, but oh, how I wish this happiness could go on forever." Emma sighed.

Martha took her hand. "I won't lie to you honey, there are rough spots ahead and you've been through so much already. When you become a Christian your past life doesn't go away. You will still have to deal with it, but when the hard times come, just place whatever is bothering you into the hands of the Lord and leave it there. It's one of the hardest things for a Christian to do. We always want to work things out for ourselves, but alone we aren't strong enough. If you need help, go to your new friends and don't hesitate to call us and we'll pray with you. There is strength in numbers."

*   *   *

Sue tucked her hand into her brother's arm as they sat watching Emma from across the room. "She positively glows tonight doesn't she? I'm so happy for her."

"She does," Jake agreed with a smile.

Just then a friend approached asking, "Susie how's the leg?" Releasing Jake she turned to speak with her friend.

Stepping away Jake pondered his sister's question. Emma radiated happiness and Jake felt a fierce desire to protect her. The sensation had been building since the first night when he'd found her alone and terrified, clutching the blanket to her in fear. As the days passed he'd been struck by her determination. When she set her mind to something nothing it seemed would stop her. Sometimes when her guard was down for a moment he'd seen the despair and loneliness shadowed in her eyes and wondered what could have hurt her so deeply. Yesterday when he had led her to Christ, was one of the happiest days of his life. One day she would have to deal with her past and all the hurt she had been through. He prayed that when the time was right, he would be there for her again.

Jake caught his breath. Feeling light headed he turned and swiftly left the room. Dodging friends and neighbors he retreated to the corral where he could come to terms with the revelation he'd just received. How could he have been so blind? Why hadn't he seen the truth staring him in the face? The impossible had happened. He was in love with Emma. He shook his head in disbelief. No one must know. Her salvation was too new, and she needed to establish her life as a Christian before he might begin to hope that she would return his love.

In love! It didn't seem possible. When Amy died,

he thought that part of his life was over for good. Now here was head over heels in love with a woman he had only known for a little over a month.

Jake realized that Emma was as different from Amy as night and day. He forced himself take a look at his situation comparing the feelings he had for Emma with those he had shared with Amy.

When he met Amy he was a country music star and she was the bass player in his band. They had been thrown into close contact while on tour, and love had blossomed almost overnight.

He'd had many responsibilities pulling at him. When their parents had died, Jake had inherited a prestigious hotel chain.

Hancock Hotels had been in his father's family for three generations, but it was Jake's father who had expanded the business to a multi-national chain of luxury Hotels. Thankfully he had set up a good board of directors to run the company. Jake had served on the board and was being groomed to take over operations when he'd had a falling out with his parents over his desire for a singing career. It was a rough time for his parents who were having trouble with Sue. It seemed that every time they turned around, Sue was in trouble.

After his parents died he became Sue's guardian and at seventeen, she had gone through a full-scale teenaged rebellion on top of every thing else. Finally, Sue had met and married Joe. The board of directors of the Hancock Hotels ran the company like a well oiled machine and except for quarterly board meetings and regular reports he had been free to pursue his singing career.

Women had always thrown themselves at him, but Amy was different she seemed to see the man that he was beneath the façade he presented to the world and they had married.

Amy had wanted a baby right away and she'd chaffed as month after month went by with no results. She'd never had any patience with the press and when she finally became pregnant she holed up in the house. He'd understood when she didn't want to tour with him, but she became so withdrawn and depressed that he'd called in specialists to help her. After Candy was born she'd gradually returned to normal.

Her mother had started taking Amy and Candy to church while he was gone and she was ecstatic the day she called to tell him she had found Jesus. While he was happy for her it hadn't meant much to him until he returned home after his tour and found his wife to be a new woman.

The next six months were wonderful. Then the day came when he'd answered the door to a policeman informing him of the death of his wife and daughter and his world had collapsed in on him.

The situation with Emma was very different; she was a contradiction of sorts. Strong enough to stand on her own, brave enough to face her fears, determined enough to carry on in the face of opposition. Personal weakness was something she would not allow, and when she found herself in his arms terrified by something she couldn't control, she had clung to him helplessly. He knew that something had happened to rob her of the joy that should have been in her life and yet she had recognized God's calling and upon receiving him she had embraced freedom with both arms. He felt that he must protect her, not only from the unforeseen problems that lay ahead, but mostly from himself.

He stood praying in the darkness seeking guidance before he returned to the party.

* * *

"Can I have your attention please? We are happy you could all come tonight. This is a momentous occasion for us. Sue has been freed from her plaster prison." Amidst applause Joe motioned for quiet. "It's a good thing she will soon be back to normal. You see in eight months she's having a baby!" Cheers and congratulations rang out and Sue beamed with pleasure.

"As a favor, Jake has agreed to sing a special song for us. Come on up here Jake."

As Jake took the stage, guitar in hand, he looked out over the crowd. "I believe the deal was that I'd sing if I had back up. Emma, come up here, you know this song." For a moment he wondered if she would come. Then she moved forward propelled by many hands patting her on the back.

Cheeks pink she delighted Jake by sitting at the keyboard where she adjusted the microphone. As they sang 'Daddy's Girl' she watched the audience. The effect was profound and left them misty-eyed. Emma knew that if she looked at Jake she would join them. When they finished, the applause was deafening.

Doc stepped forward, grinning widely, and passed them a soundtrack of a popular duet Jake had recorded with a well-known female artist.

"Don't worry, she knows it," he assured Jake as he put it in the machine.

With a look of admonishment at Doc, Emma brought her microphone to the middle of the stage stood with Jake. When the music started she whispered, "If you listen closely, you'll discover one of my secrets tonight."

Jake gave her a curious glance and began to sing. The song, a slow ballad, featured a man and woman asking each other if true love lasts forever. Often, performers made small changes to the music. When it was her turn to sing, Emma sang the song as she had written it and not as the woman who had performed it. She knew that Jake's quick mind would know the difference.

Emma watched Jake as she began to sing and she grinned when he almost missed his cue as it dawned on him who she was. The song was soon over and they laughingly bowed off the stage declining to sing an encore.

Recorded music filled the air and many couples returned to the dance floor. Drawing her arm through his Jake asked solemnly. "May I have this dance?"

A bubble of laughter escaped her as she nodded in assent. He took her in his arms oblivious to the many eyes following them.

"So, Miss Emma, are you really Jeri Forester, or is Jeri Forester really you?"

"Jeri Forester is really me. Only my producer Greg Paulson, my family and now you, know my secret."

"I know Greg, he's a friend of mine. 'Daddy's Girl' won a lot of awards, including best songwriter. Your songs win awards every year. Why aren't you there to receive them?"

"At first I was too young. I sent my first tape to Greg when I was fourteen. The first award I received was right after my parents died and I decided to keep my identity a secret." Changing the subject, she said. "You know, I have at least six CD's in my cabin with your name on them. You haven't been accepting them and they are starting to pile up."

"Is the clutter getting to you?" He asked with a wry grin.

"Sure, could you take them off my hands?"

"Maybe, but, I'm not sure I want to continue with my career."

"The choice is yours to make," she said seriously. "Just take the CD's; you are the only one who can do the songs justice." He looked puzzled so she explained how the music came, and why sending the songs to another artist wouldn't work.

"I know you caused quite a stir in the music industry insisting on certain artists no matter what record label they worked under. Producers don't usually share music with other recording companies. It must be wonderful to have such a gift," he sighed.

"Sometimes it's a gift, and sometimes a curse. When your down and depressed, you don't want a happy little song rattling around your head." With a thoughtful look she continued. "There were times when I'd have done almost anything to make it stop. I think I've sent every kind of music you can think of to Greg at one time or another."

The music ended and as they left the dance floor he assured her. "Your secret's safe with me."

"What secret's that?"

Emma hadn't noticed Romeo come in. His arm was around the waist of an uncomfortable looking young redhead and he had obviously been drinking.

"Now if I told you, it wouldn't be a secret anymore, would it?" She asked lightly. "Are you going to introduce us to your friend?"

"Sure, this here's Penny Malone. That's Jake an'

Emma."

Emma had lived with fear for too long not to recognize it in Penny's eyes. The girl was definitely in over her head. "We were just heading for something to eat. Would you like to join us?" She offered.

"That would be nice, I am hungry." Penny glanced at Romeo. "Do you mind?"

"Lead me to it; I'm a bit hollow myself."

After helping themselves at the buffet table, they found a place to sit and Romeo started eating.

"Do you live here in town Penny?" Jake asked.

"Yes. My Mom runs the Last Chance Cafe on Main Street."

"They have good food there," Jake commented.

Penny blushed, "Thanks, I do a lot of the cooking as well as waiting on tables."

"That's how we met," explained Romeo. As he launched into the story of how they met, Emma noticed that the food was having the desired effect on Romeo. The effects of the alcohol seemed to be lessening and she wondered if Penny was afraid of him or the situation.

"If you gentlemen will excuse me I'll step to the ladies room and freshen up. Coming Penny?" With that she successfully whisked Penny away.

Making sure they were alone. Emma gently drew the girl out. Romeo's good looks and attention had flattered her, and the promise of a party at the Lazy J had sounded exciting. Romeo was a nice guy and they had fun before he'd started drinking.

Emma asked her if she would be more comfortable staying at the ranch. "Oh no, I couldn't I have to work tomorrow so I'd better get back."

"I could arrange a ride if you think Romeo's had a little more to drink than he should."

"Could you? I would really appreciate it. I was afraid to let him drive me home." The relief showing in her eyes spoke volumes.

After making arrangements with a local couple to take Penny home, the girls returned to the table and Penny claimed tiredness and an early morning as her reason to leave.

Romeo having sobered considerably agreed and walked her to the car.

Later, when everyone had left, Emma hung up her apron and looked around the clean kitchen. The local women had helped with the clean up. The torches were snuffed and the candles extinguished, everything was in its place. The few guests that were staying over had retired to their cabins. Jake walked in as Emma switched off the lights and turned to go.

"I thought you might need these," he said handing

her a bundle. "I hope you don't mind that I used my key."

Emma exclaimed in delight over socks, jogging shoes and her warm jacket. "Thank you, I could really use these." Switching the kitchen lights on she hurriedly got into her gear.

"My feet are saying 'ahhh' how did you ever think of this?"

"'Elementary my dear Watson.'" Jake quoted. "Your sandals, though pretty, aren't what you're used to and although the wrap is a perfect match for the dress, it's thin and the night air is chilly."

"Trust a man to take the illusion out of a situation," she laughed.

There was a strange light in his eyes as he said cryptically. "I don't think that's possible. Are you ready?"

"Yes sir," she curtseyed, then looking down at her shoes she laughed.

This time it was he who switched off the lights as they left the building. The moon illuminated the path as they walked in companionable silence.

At last Emma broke the quiet. "What did you say to Romeo while Penny and I were gone?"

Remembering the lecture he'd given him on drunk driving, he glossed over the truth a bit. "Oh, not much. We just talked."

"Shore," she drawled, mimicking Ken. "Am I supposed to believe that?"

"Of course," he laughed.

Emma smiled; she liked the way his laugh rolled up from deep within him. It gave her a warm feeling inside. Chill bumps stood up on her arms whenever she heard it.

"This has been a perfect night. I can't remember when I've enjoyed my self so much," she smiled.

Climbing the porch steps she asked him not to go away as she dashed inside. Returning almost immediately she handed him the bundle of CD's and sheet music from her shelf. "Please take them, they're yours." She said simply.

Looking into her moonlit eyes he would have walked across hot coals if she'd asked him to. He tucked the bundle under his arm and nodded, not trusting himself to speak.

"Thank-you." She said simply and on impulse reached out and placed her hand gently on his cheek, then withdrew it quickly placing it over her pounding heart.

Confused by the charged atmosphere and the electric sensation of his slightly rough face against her palm, she stared at him wide-eyed for a long moment. There was a vulnerable light in his eyes and something that both stirred and frightened her. The intimacy of the situation suddenly struck her.

She hadn't deliberately touched a man in such a manner in over five years. Yet here she was, wanting his touch more than she wanted air to breathe.

Murmuring, "Good night," she turned and went swiftly into the cabin where she locked the door and leaned against it shaking like a leaf. Her fingers still tingled from their contact. Breathing deeply she forced herself across the room on unsteady legs, and fell into a chair. Pulling up her knees, she wrapped her arms around them and buried her face trying to make sense of what had just happened.

Jake as, always, had been a perfect gentleman, she could never fault him. In fact he was nearly perfect in every way. Whether up to his elbows in soap bubbles scrubbing a grimy pot, gentling a fractious child or bucking hay bales in the barn. He did everything with quiet dignity, and his smile- his smile was incredible.

What was she doing? She hadn't thought like this about a man's smile since college. Emotions she'd kept dammed up for years came rushing in, washing away barriers and leaving her trembling in their wake. She'd had schoolgirl crushes before, and dated in college, but after the incident with Carl she had shut the door firmly on that part of her life. It had been years until she'd forced herself to date, but even then she wouldn't allow a man to touch her. Let alone want to touch him.

Love was an emotion she hadn't allowed herself to

feel since that day in the operating room when the remnants of her world had come crashing down around her.

Remembering that Dr. Hanson had said it would be better for the baby if she was given a spinal block and remained awake during the surgery, she once again recalled her nervousness. She had waited quietly while the skilled surgeon had done his best to repair the defect in Angel's tiny heart.

Once again she felt the terror that assailed her when Angel's heart had stopped. The doctors and nurses had done everything humanly possible even fully removing Angel from the womb, but they couldn't save her.

Doc had been there. He had been crying, she remembered that his tears had made wet spots on his surgical mask.

"Please Jim, keep trying," he had begged, picking up the tiny body which Emma saw again with startling clarity. Angel had been small for being in the sixth month of life; she was barely longer than Doc's hand.

"There's nothing I can do," the surgeon had said gently. "Nothing, if only-"he'd broken off.

Emma's mind finished his thoughts, if only she had come in earlier, if only she hadn't kept her pregnancy a secret, if only she had received proper medical treatment. If only…

"No-o-o!"

There had been an unearthly cry. A sound that rose up from the emptiness inside her, bursting forth before she even realized she had made it. Struggling to make her paralyzed body move she'd tried to get to Angel, tried to reach out to her daughter.

"Oh no! Put her out, put her out!" Doc had cried. Then a blinding pain ripped through her and darkness had descended.

Emma prayed until late into the night, trying her best to leave everything in the hands of the Lord.

Chapter 6

Emma shook her head as she tried to untangle what had once been a neat harness. She was cleaning the tack room and had found the mess in a corner.

"Don't waste yo're time on it. I don't think anyone could make sense of it." Ken stood in the doorway watching her struggle.

"I wonder if it would help to rub some oil into it." She thought out loud as she fought with the stiff leather.

"Couldn't hurt, here try this," he suggested, handing her some neat's-foot oil.

He watched for a while as she worked the oil into the leather straps. Then he said thoughtfully. "You know Miss Emma, peoples lives are a lot like that there harness. Things happen, sometimes things you have no say in, and you get all twisted up and dry as a bone, but when you apply a little oil of the spirit it softens you and slowly the knots fall away."

While he spoke, the knots slowly unraveled, leaving a useful piece of equipment where once there had been a useless mess.

Emma smiled at the older man and observed. "I

believe you've hit the nail on the head. When our lives are tangled and dry, like this harness was, we aren't much good to God, but when we let Him soften and unravel us he can put us to use again." She thought for a moment. "You've made me realize just how twisted up my life's been. God has poured down his spirit, but how do I begin to untangle the mess I've made of it?"

Looking up at him she seemed humbled and in need of direction. He drew a deep breath and with a prayer for guidance, he said. "I don't know what's happened in yo're past. All I know is, sometimes God allows things to happen to you, so's you can help somebody who's goin' through the same thing. If you see somebody a headin' for a 'knot' you can steer 'em clear of the same hurtin' you've had."

"'Course, there are some tangles God makes on purpose. He weaves our lives together for a reason. Like bringin' you here, yo're life's all tangled up with ours now, an' no matter where you go you'll always be a part of us here, and you'll always be tangled up in our hearts. I guess it's up to you to find out which knots need untanglin'. Maybe you should just take hold of the end of yo're problem and work backwards." He scratched his balding head and asked. "Does that make any sense?"

"I believe it does." Emma smiled. "Thanks Ken, I'm afraid I'm about as good at being a Christian as I am at ranching. It's all new to me."

"Yo're catchin' on just fine, Missy and don't let

anyone tell you no different." With a nod he left her to her thoughts.

The weeks since the party had been busy. Sue was getting around pretty well now and Emma wondered how much longer she would be needed. They had asked her to stay on and that was fine with her. The thought of leaving brought a lump to her throat. Leaving the ranch held no allure for her. She had come to consider it her home.

After the party she had forced herself to act normally around Jake. Soon she was able to once again relax and enjoy their friendship, though every day she felt more and more drawn to him.

"Start from the end and go backwards." Ken had said. She thought back over her time here at the ranch. She had learned so much, and her life had changed drastically.

Thinking over the last five years, she realized that she had allowed herself to become more and more bitter and reclusive as the years had gone by. She was slowly coming to terms with her bitterness and wondered how God could possibly be able to use something so ugly to help someone else? Shaking her head she went to make supper.

The next day Penny surprised her by stopping in after lunch. "I'm sorry I haven't come by before now. I wanted to thank you again for helping me at the party."

"No problem." Emma welcomed her with a smile.

"I've been in some rough places before myself. Have you eaten?"

"I ate with Mom at the restaurant before I came."

"You must bring your Mother with you next time you come. I'd like to meet her." She poured iced tea and set out a plate of cookies.

"Are you sure I'm not keeping you from your work?" Penny asked, concern showing in her big blue eyes.

"I have about thirty minutes before Katie comes. If you aren't in a hurry I'd like you to meet her." Emma told her about the engaging child.

"That would be great I love kids. What do you do with them?"

Emma explained how the therapy worked. "We don't just deal with the disability, we address the whole child. Some of these children have been brought up in an almost sterile environment. It's good for them to come to a working ranch. They come into contact with all sorts of animals and new experiences." Heavens she sounded like Sue. She understood with perfect clarity how Joe and Sue felt, and why it meant so much to them to get this camp up and running.

Glancing at her watch, she suggested they head to the stables.

Katie and Penny hit it off immediately and Penny was an invaluable help, she seemed to know what was needed before she was asked.

After Katie left. Penny took her leave with a promise to return soon."

Emma smiled to herself she liked Penny. She had noticed how the girl kept glancing around as if she were looking for someone. There must be a lot more to Romeo than met the eye.

"A penny for your thoughts." Jake offered with a twinkle in his eye.

"Too late, you just missed her," she laughed, then sobered. "I hope Romeo knows what a treasure she is."

"He talks of nothing else, the boys have been riding him pretty hard, and even though he tries to keep up his bad boy image, I think he's smitten.

"He could do far worse than Penny Malone. I like her, Jake. It frightens me to think of what might have happened the night of the party." There was a shadow of worry in her eyes.

"I don't think we have to worry too much about his drinking. Joe took him to task pretty hard and he swears it won't happen again."

Emma added a fervent. "I hope not."

Changing the subject Jake asked. "How's your music career coming along?"

"Great. I don't think I've ever done such good

work. It makes me want to upgrade my equipment. The backgrounds are still too synthesized."

"What are you using now?"

"Come and see," she invited. "There's a melody I'd like to get recorded."

They talked shop as they walked companionably side by side. "You know," she glanced at him speculatively, "I could use some help on this song, if you don't mind, you could bring your guitar."

"I'd like that," Jake smiled.

They stopped long enough to pick up his instrument on the way to her cabin. Unlocking the door she said. "Make yourself comfortable, I want to wash up a bit."

"I'll use the kitchen sink, if you don't mind."

"Go right ahead. I won't be a minute."

"Sure, that's what they all say." He laughed.

Making a face she took herself off to clean up.

True to her word she came back in record time. Then she led the way into the sound room where she switched on the power and started flipping switches and turning knobs.

She showed him her rack of compact disks and tapes.

"This is an impressive set up." Jake whistled. "Why

are these marked 'unknown'?"

"I know it sounds strange, but sometimes I don't recognize the artist singing in my head. When that happens I set it aside and wait until I hear their voice on the radio."

They plugged his guitar into the system and she filled him in on the technical aspects of the music. With the key, tempo and style determined, they settled down to work, or perhaps struggle would be a better word for it. Finally she shook her head and admitted it wasn't working. "I'm sorry; I'm not used to an audience."

Jake moved his stool over to her side and sat out of her direct line of vision. "Don't think about me. Take a deep breath and let the music flow. It'll come."

Emma let his velvet voice run over her, she wasn't so sure she could ignore him. Somehow he was as much a part of this piece of music as he was a part of her life. Tangled lives, Ken had said.

Closing her eyes she let her fingers run over the keys and before long she knew where the music was going. The melody began to flow and take shape, but the lyrics were patchy. Why, of course! Why hadn't she thought of that before?

Turning to look directly at him she spoke. "When I was in college, my roommate and I used to write songs together, usually duets, I got part of the lyrics, and she got the other." He listened attentively, and she wondered how he would react to the next bit of news. "That's what's happening now."

For a long moment time stood still. Looking into each other's eyes no words were necessary. The air around them was charged with electricity and Jake spoke two words.

"Let's go."

The music poured from her fingertips and through his guitar. The words flowed between them like a whirlwind of thought and sound, rising ever higher. Pulling them along until reaching the end they were left suspended in time and space. The music softly died away leaving the last line hanging in the air between them.

"Forever and always we'll not be apart, God's tangled our lives, and He's tangled our hearts."

They were silent. Emma drew a tremulous breath. Eyes locked, Jake set his guitar aside and standing extended his raised hands. Reaching out, she placed her hands against his, palms together. Linking their fingers they stood their eyes asking questions neither could voice.

Releasing her hands, he drew her into his arms and she knew without a doubt she was finally home. The knowledge of her love for him rocked her. No wonder she wasn't afraid to be close to him, to let him hold her, she trusted him completely. With her eyes closed she breathed in the scent of him warm and alive, and she never wanted to let him go. Her heart thundered in her chest and she could feel the beating of his against her cheek. Was it possible that he felt the same?

She lifted her head and the sweetness in her tear filled eyes gave his heart wings. Gently his lips met hers in a kiss as soft as a spring breeze. Their lips parted on a sigh and cupping her face in his hands, Jake gently wiped the tears from her eyes. Then with a groan, he pulled her once more into his embrace.

"Don't cry," he murmured into the curling tendrils of hair at her temple.

"I can't help it," with a look of amazement on her face she shyly raised her eyes to his. "I've never felt like this before."

There was pain on his face as he asked. "Are you sure you're not just feeling 'the magic of the moment'?"

With a thoughtful look she said. "I've felt that magic many times. This is the same magic that has been with me since the morning you burst into my bedroom to rescue me."

The brilliant smile that dawned on her face and was mirrored on his, "Thank God." He breathed.

Minutes flew by as hand in hand they asked their Heavenly Father for guidance and patience, to wait on Him, as they struggled to keep him the center of their lives.

Chapter 7

Slightly diluted music drifted through the telephone receiver. Why did they play music while you were on hold, she wondered? She had already been through this with her lawyer's office and here she was holding again.

Emma's mind wandered a thousand miles away. Jake had been gone three days and she missed him terribly. He'd insisted on calling her every night and was ecstatic over the progress of the new album he was recording. After working on 'Tangled Hearts' he had confessed that he'd been negotiating a contract for a new album, a mixture of country and gospel. He had needed one more song and 'Tangled' Hearts was perfect. It had taken him some time and a lot of prayer to convince her to sing with him on the album. Finally she'd admitted the music had come to her in her own voice, not that of another, and she agreed to sing. She was sure it was no coincidence they had the same producer.

Greg Paulson came on the line. "Emma, sorry to keep you waiting. John's new album is incredible. I'm glad you met him and convinced him to come back to work."

"All I did was give him some CD's I hadn't sent in

yet." Emma acknowledged. "The rest was up to him."

"Well, whatever you did, it was brilliant. He's very close-lipped about 'Tangled Hearts'. It's a wonderful number. I want to release it as a single, if the same energy comes off in the studio as is on that recording, I'm sure it'll go platinum!"

"I don't know about platinum, but I know it's good."

"You've always doubted your impact on people Emma." He said seriously. "It's time to come out of the shadows and receive the recognition you deserve."

"Right now let's concentrate on the project at hand," she said dryly. "When will you need me there?"

"At the rate John's going I'd say the end of next week. He has always had unbelievable concentration, but this new album has an entirely different feel to it and he's getting through it in record time."

"That's great, I'm glad it's going well." Emma replied.

"There's something else I need to know," he paused for a moment. "What name you'll be singing under?"

"Oh,' she groaned. " I hadn't thought about that."

"You see Jeri Forester is a big name in this business and the mystery that surrounds you is sure to sell albums."

Emma understood what he was getting at. "If I allow my name on the album, you think it'll sell better," she said flatly.

"Now before you put that wall up and call the whole thing off, I want you to think about what a hit like this would do for John Tabor. Oh, I know a return album from him will sell, but an album with the reclusive Jeri Forester could put him over the top."

Goodness, did everyone notice the walls she'd hid behind for so long?

"You're going to push this angle, aren't you?" There was resignation in her voice.

Hearing her weakening he pressed gently. "Only if you'll let me."

"You're good," she acknowledged. "Okay, But he gets all the interviews. I'm involved in name only. No pictures, no interviews."

She gave him specific instructions on how she wanted the contracts worded.

"You got it sweetheart. I'll have the contracts drawn and ready by the time you get here next Thursday. You do realize this will be the first time I've seen you face to face."

"I'll try to hide my warts," she laughed.

Greg Paulson was a whiz at getting temperamental artists to agree with him. Emma shook her head and smiled. Something kept tickling the back of her mind. She couldn't believe that she, Emma Winters, had enough impact on people to make much of a difference, but perhaps Jeri Forester did. She was going to need to pray more about the tenuous plan beginning to take form.

Picking up the phone she placed a call to her banker.

* * *

"When will you be back?" Sue asked.

"As soon as we're finished recording. It shouldn't be more than a few days. Jake's moving through the songs quickly and I have a feeling this will move fast too." Jake had left their song till last so they could fly home together when it was finished.

"Take the whole week. You deserve a break. I'm glad you and Jake are working together," she said with a grin then asked. "Are you in love with him?" At Emma's gasp she continued. "Go ahead and tell me it's none of my business, but I can't help seeing the way you look at him when you think no one's watching."

Emma felt herself blushing. "I think so," she grinned.

"Oh, Emma I'm so happy for you," she cried and threw her arms around her friend. "Have you told him?"

"No- well, I'm not even sure about this yet."

"Well, has he told you?" Sue asked confused.

"The subject hasn't come up. Quit worrying everything will work out eventually." Emma assured her.

Chattering happily they were finishing lunch clean up when, without warning, Sue turned slightly green and dove for the crackers and clear soda she kept on the counter.

"Are you going to be okay?" Emma asked. "Penny said she would cook as well as work with the kids."

"I'll be fine, but I will take her up on the cooking. Doc says the morning sickness will pass. I just wish it wouldn't last all day," she said with a grimace.

Emma shuddered. "Morning sickness is awful. Just when you think you can handle it, your stomach revolts. It's worse if you don't keep some food in you, even if you can't keep it down."

Shaking her head, Sue marveled at how perceptive Emma was. How could she speak with such familiarity unless she had been pregnant herself? - Oh my, that would explain a lot. She had seen the way Emma watched her with troubled eyes and, always asked if everything was all right after her visits to Doc. Burning with curiosity Sue decided she wouldn't pry; she would wait until Emma was ready to talk about it. Instead she continued. "I'm sure Penny and I will get along fine. Want to make a guess who will volunteer for dish duty?"

"Romeo," they chorused together.

Joe walked in to the sounds of laughter. "Now that's a pretty picture. My favorite brunette and my favorite blonde getting along famously."

Ducking the dishtowel she threw at him, he caught Sue around the waist. "I like not having to run to catch you," he teased as she took another swipe at him.

"You never had to run to catch me. All you had to do was make me mad enough and I chased you!"

Emma had heard rumors about their tempestuous courtship. You would never know it now, but they had gotten off to a rather rough start.

"I'm glad I have you both here. There's something on my mind I'd like to talk about. Let's get some iced tea and sit down."

When they were seated Emma took a deep breath. "You already know that I was in a band in college, but there are a few things you don't know about me. Jake's not the only one who's been living a double life. Doc told you I work for a sound studio. That's partly right, I'm a songwriter. I write under the name Jeri Forester."

"Jeri Forester! Jake's been singing your praises for years. You wrote 'Daddy's Girl' and tons of other songs. No wonder you were able to do that duet with Jake at the party." Sue enthused. "He was always excited when he got one of your CD's in the mail because he knew it would be a hit." She stopped wide-eyed. "As far as I know no one has ever seen you."

"You can see why I don't want anyone to know who I am." Emma chuckled.

"Yes, the press would be all over you." Sue turned thoughtful. "You know, Amy tried to be patient with the media but she wasn't able to handle the pressure. Then when they sneaked into the hospital to take pictures of the baby she went ballistic. I tried to get her to cooperate with the reporters. Schedule a press conference and give them what they want so they'd leave them alone, but she'd have no part in it." Sue sighed.

"Jake did everything he could to shield her, but she hated it. If you ever decide to go public, don't get frustrated with the press. Just think of it as free publicity." Her eyes told Emma, more than her words, that there would come a time when she must face the outside world. Emma knew reporters could be ruthless when on the trail of a story.

"Thanks for the good advice, I'll remember it."

Joe spoke up. "Are you worried that some reporter on Jake's trail will find you out?"

"That's a possibility I've thought about. I'll cross that bridge when I get there." There was a quiet strength about her and Joe and Sue knew she wouldn't cave under pressure.

"What I really want to tell you is that I want all proceeds from my portion of 'Tangled Hearts' to go to the ranch."

The stunned silence ended abruptly, as Joe and Sue tripped over each other spluttering in protest.

Emma raised her hands to quiet them. "Don't argue about it, my mind is made up. You need equipment, a gym, pool, sauna, wheelchair accessible walkways and ramps," she ticked each item off with her fingers, "and that's just for the kids. I don't know how much money 'Tangled hearts' will bring in, but my producer Greg bets it'll go platinum."

She raised a finger as the protests began anew. "The arrangements have already been made the money will be sent to a trust set up to fund the ranch. You don't have to use it, but it will just sit there if you don't."

"Em we can't take your money. I know you aren't making that much from your job here." Sue protested.

Emma grinned, "'Tangled Hearts' isn't my first hit and I don't 'need' to work. I came here because Doc convinced me you needed help. I stayed because I love this place. Let me help make your dream come true, not just for you, but also for the kids and their parents."

Joe and Sue looked at each other hope dawning in

their eyes as their dream drew closer to reality.

* * *

The plane taxied to the terminal. "Welcome to Nashville International Airport please stay in your seat until we have made a complete stop..." The flight attendant was busy helping passengers with their preparations for departure. Emma took a deep breath and let it out slowly.

"Your first flight?" The white haired woman sitting next to her asked.

"No. I'm just excited to be here," she smiled.

"Nashville is a beautiful city. Keep your eye out for singing stars you don't always recognize them in street clothes. Once someone snapped my picture mistaking me for Loretta Lynn," the woman chuckled. "I'm Natalie Grey," she introduced herself and held out her hand.

"Emma Winters," taking the woman's hand in hers, she grinned. "Thanks for the warning."

As she walked down the tunnel her heart raced. Emerging with the other passengers she scanned the waiting crowd for a familiar face. It was after six o'clock but she wasn't sure if Jake had finished working and would be able to meet her.

"Emma." A hand touched her arm and that wonderful velvet voice reached out to her. She turned in surprise as Jake clad in an expensive cut business suit put his arm around her and whisked her out of the flow of exiting passengers.

A look of amazement on her face she grinned. "Natalie Grey was right. I didn't recognize you at first."

"Who?" Jake asked confused.

Quickly she explained about the kind woman on the plane. Her eyes were animated and she posed a lovely picture. As Jake stared at her drinking his fill with his eyes, he realized they were beginning to draw attention.

He dropped a kiss on her upturned lips and smiled. "Let's get out of here." As they turned to go a camera flashed. Feeling Jake stiffen she instinctively placed her hand on his arm. Emma blinked at the woman she had sat next to on the flight.

Mrs. Grey smiled, waving a cheap camera. "See," she laughed. "You never know when you'll be mistaken for a celebrity."

"I don't think anyone would mistake me for Loretta Lynn." Emma laughed. "But, keep that picture. You never know what could happen."

A small child ran up calling, "Grandma, Grandma."

Waving good-bye they headed for the baggage claim area. She explained the woman's comments to Jake on the way.

With a wry grimace he explained, "I thought it was

reporters at first. I was ready to tell them to take a hike, when I realized it was the woman you told me about. Too bad my knight in shining armor routine wasn't necessary."

"I like your knight in shining armor routine," she teased.

Having claimed her luggage they made their way to his rented car, and were soon on the way to the hotel.

"Sue told me about the problems you've had in the past with the press," she told him. "Don't worry I know my secret will come out eventually. I would like to remain anonymous for awhile longer, but meanwhile, I'm enjoying your disguise. I like the suit," she smiled appreciatively.

"This is a disguise of sorts. When I am in the city, I dress like a businessman. I'm less conspicuous like this."

"Believe me, you'll never be inconspicuous. No matter what you wear, women will always notice," she said dryly.

"You're rather spectacular yourself, you know. I saw two men run into the wall while watching you, and no less than four women elbow their husbands for looking at you."

"You're exaggerating, but I love it," Emma laughed.

He had not exaggerated. Jake had been impatient to

get her out of the airport. She was stunning in that light blue dress. Remembering her reaction to Romeo, he had wanted to shield her from the possibility that someone might offend her. And here she was trying to defend him.

Soon they were walking into the Hancock Hotel. Approaching the desk Jake asked for Miss Winter's key. After signing the registration card, they were escorted to the elevator by a uniformed bellman, and whisked to the penthouse. Leaving Emma's bags in her bedroom and being assured they would call on him if they needed anything else. Jake tipped the bellman and he bowed out. Leaving them alone in the sitting room.

Emma raised her eyebrows. "The penthouse?" She asked.

"Greg often puts celebrities up here. It's the executive suite. I hope you don't mind. My room is over here." He motioned to a door on the opposite side of the room.

"That's fine with me. It's still within screaming distance if I need a knight in shining armor," she joked.

Bowing deeply he said dramatically. "At your service M' Lady."

"Thank-you kind sir," she replied with a curtsy.

Their laughter broke the slight tension in the air caused by the unfamiliar surroundings.

"Would you prefer to go out for supper or order from room service?" Jake asked.

"Room service, if you don't mind," she said promptly. "I'm a little tired, and we have to be at the studio early tomorrow morning."

"Here is the menu, what would you like."

"Anything I don't have to cook," she smiled.

"That means fondue is out," he teased.

"I'll unpack, just don't order anything raw."

"Sushi's out." he laughed. "I guess its steak. At least I know you like it medium rare." As he lifted the phone, she went to her room.

They ate on the terrace. The steak was cooked to perfection. Caesar salad, steamed asparagus and fluffy baked potatoes were followed by cherry cheesecake.

Lingering over their coffee Emma told Jake her plans to donate her proceeds from Tangled Hearts to the ranch.

Jake shook his head and grinned. "We think alike. Now Joe and Sue are getting all the proceeds from the song," he smiled explaining that he had done the same thing. "I wonder if we should combine our trust accounts."

"That might be a good idea. It could get confusing." She hid a yawn behind her hand.

"What do you say to an early night?" He asked concerned.

"I think that's a good idea, it's been a long day. Sue insisted on shopping in Denver. I'm afraid she's been saving her energy since she's been laid up."

"You must be weary. Susie in a shopping mall is an exhausting experience," he grinned.

After the dinner dishes had been removed. They settled down in the sitting room. It had become a habit to pray together before retiring for the night, and they saw no reason not to do so now.

Chapter 8

Pete the uniformed guard knew Jake and opened the door as they approached. "Good morning Mr. Tabor," he welcomed them with a smile to Paulson Records, Greg's recording studio.

Deciding that Saturday morning would be the best time to avoid notice, Greg had set up the recording session with as few people involved as possible. The woman behind the reception desk waved them toward the bank of elevators.

Soon they were speaking to Greg's receptionist, "Go right in Mr. Tabor." she said, glancing curiously at Emma.

Jake opened the door and ushered Emma inside.

The corner office was tastefully decorated; the view of the Nashville skyline was spectacular, but it was the man sitting behind the desk that held Emma's interest. Greg Paulson a tall man in his fifties wore a look of stunned disbelief on his handsome features. As if coming out of a trance, he shook his head, and rising from his chair, he came around the desk to take her hands in his.

"Emma?" there was a question in his voice as he

openly stared into her face taking in the her delicate features and slender body encased in a sky blue dress that flared gently at the knees.

"Hello Greg, it's good to finally meet you," she said with a twinkle in her eye.

"It really is you. I'd know that voice anywhere," he smiled. Releasing her hands he motioned to comfortable chairs. "Have a seat, and let me look at you."

"I don't mean to embarrass you," he said as she blushed, "but, John wouldn't tell me anything about you and with all the insistence on no pictures, well-"he broke off clearly flustered.

"You thought I had two heads and a very large nose," she laughed lightening the situation.

Jake grinned. "In all the years I've known you, Greg, I don't believe I've ever seen you at a loss for words."

They all laughed, and the tension in the room eased.

"Are you ready to get down to business?"

"Yes I am as soon as we get a few things straightened out." Explaining how they both wanted the money from 'Tangled Hearts' allocated, they got down to business and signed the contracts.

"Studio three is clear, you know the way John. I'll be sitting in on the taping." Rising he shook Emma's hand and led them to the door.

Jake and Emma stood in the sound proof studio, they were both wearing headphones. Microphones and music stands were set up in front of them.

"Okay the sound check is great and we're ready when you are." Greg's voice came over the headphones. Emma took a deep breath, hands clasped she turned to Jake, her nervousness was evident.

"Just a minute." Jake spoke to Greg and the technicians. Moving the music stands to the side, he set the microphones so they could face each other. One more quick sound check and they were ready.

Tom the technician gave the go ahead and music filled the headphones. Jake had asked him to play the soundtrack completely through first, and then give them a moment before starting the recording.

When the music started Emma closed her eyes and let the melody roll over her. By the end of the first verse she was smiling and her mouth was moving with the music. When the last note died away Jake reached out and, as was their custom at home, they held hands and bowed their heads in prayer.

"Father," he prayed, "we come before you with humbled hearts, waiting on your presence."

"Allow us, "Emma continued, "to show others the love you have for them, may their lives and hearts become tangled with yours."

Together they said, "Amen."

Greg held his breath and waited. As the music began he watched the couple on the other side of the glass. It was easy to see they were in a world all their own, a place where he and the sound crew could not intrude.

As the music rose and fell, the haunting melody filled the booth taking them to heights they never knew they could achieve. The hardened technicians and Greg found tears in their eyes as the music faded away.

Jake and Emma stood, hands clasped, eyes closed, oblivious to all. Trembling, Emma fell in his arms tears running unchecked down her cheeks. As he held her Jake raised his eyes to heaven in a prayer of thanksgiving.

Greg switched off the sound and turned away, giving them some privacy.

Tom looked at Greg with red eyes and took a deep breath. "This will go platinum overnight."

Chapter 9

"No wonder you wouldn't talk about 'Tangled Hearts'. To have that much energy in one place is incredible" Greg smiled at Jake and Emma. They were back in his office. "The technicians are working on it now; it's remarkable to get such a clean run on the first time through. The entire album has the same feel about it, but this song is strong enough to stand alone."

"I want to pre-release 'Tangled Hearts', we can get it to our test stations immediately. It could be on the air nation wide no later than Monday." Greg looked seriously at Jake and Emma. "I think we need to move quickly on this one."

There was a knock at the door and the receptionist handed Greg a compact disk. Thanking her he put it in a machine and pressed play. As the music began Jake and Emma's voices were heard in prayer then continued in song.

"We couldn't get away from that prayer; we had to put it in. Tom looped the first few bars of music to accommodate it." Greg looked at them pleading. "I know it was a very personal moment, but the song's not complete without it. Please say you'll let it stay?"

Taking Emma's hand Jake said, "This is your decision Em."

A shy smile washed over her features as she said, "I don't want it any other way. God gave us the song, we need to give Him the glory."

Greg cleared his throat, "It's settled then, we'll get right on it." Dialing the phone he spoke into it. "We've got the go ahead, print it as is."

Standing, he shook hands with them "Emma, it's been a pleasure. I can't tell you how much I've enjoyed meeting you at last. I want to hear more of your work. "

Turning to Jake and placing a hand on his shoulder he said. "I know you've had a rough couple of years, but I can see that you'll make it just fine."

Emma saw the mutual respect and friendship between the two men. She knew Greg Paulson had stood by and waited patiently for Jake to work through his problems even though it had cost him a lot of money. He had once done the same for her.

"Greg, I never thanked you for not pushing me when I quit for awhile. I appreciate it more than you'll ever know." The sincerity in her voice caught at his heart.

"When I called Dr. Linden, he told me you'd been quite ill and had needed surgery. He said it would be awhile before you would be able to work. I heard your recovery in your songs, and now look at you," he smiled. "More beautiful than I could imagine." As she blushed. He told Jake to be good to her or he'd come and steal her away.

Emma laughed away his nonsense and they took their leave.

*   *   *

Emma studied her reflection in the full-length mirror. Jake had asked her to wear the royal blue satin dress tonight. They were going out to celebrate. Dabbing on her favorite perfume, she made a face in the mirror and spun a pirouette. She wore her hair in a French twist from which wispy tendrils escaped curling around her face. The diamond heart earrings and necklace she had received for high school graduation, fit perfectly above the neckline of her dress.

Catching up her wrap and matching bag, she stepped into the sitting room. Jake turned and her breath caught in her throat. He was incredibly handsome, his still damp hair curled rebelliously, away from the collar of his evening clothes. The crisp white shirt was a startling contrast to his deep tan. There was a confident air about him as if he were accustomed to wearing evening clothes. Emma felt he was, by far, the most handsome man she had ever seen.

Jake's eyes took in every aspect of her with approval. Taking a deep shaky breath he asked himself, 'what have I gotten myself into?' Out loud he said, "We'd better get going, our reservation is at eight and I'm unsure of the traffic."

The restaurant was busy, but with their reservation they got right in. They were seated near the dance floor by a uniformed maitre d', who made a show of pulling out their chairs and presenting the menus with a flourish.

After he left them, Jake rolled his eyes at Emma and they tried to hold back their laughter. They enjoyed a wonderful meal of grilled salmon fillets with herbed red potatoes, crusty hot rolls, and spinach salad with vinaigrette dressing. Emma declined dessert claiming that if she wanted to get into her jeans again, she'd better quit while she was ahead. Jake made a show of looking her over and declared that she could do with a little meat on her bones.

"You could do with some exercise too. Would you care to dance?"

"I thought you'd never ask," she grinned as she used the old cliché.

Jake led her to the dance floor where she was reminded what a good dancer he was. He held her comfortably, not too close, and she was grateful. After executing a tricky bit of footwork he asked. "Where did you learn to dance like this?"

"My parents were members of the country club when I was a young teen, I took lessons there. How about you?"

"Amy and I took lessons when we were dating. She

wanted us to know something besides the Texas two step."

Walking back to the table she was laughing up at him when a camera flashed. The photographer grinned, "John Tabor, I thought it was you."

"Mike Mason, what are you doing here?" Jake asked stiffening.

"Looking for beautiful people, and finding one. Are you going to introduce me?"

"No. And I'd appreciate you not using that picture."

"Sorry, no can do. I need my bread and butter too."

Emma's hand on his arm stopped Jake from advancing. She smiled politely. "Please excuse us Mr. Mason, we have a previous engagement and must leave, but it was nice meeting you." Sailing past him she collected her things from the table and they left.

Opening her car door Jake caught her hand and kissed it. "Thank-you," he said, and she was warmed through by his smile.

As they drove back to the hotel Emma commented, "I hope you realize I don't intend to run away from every reporter we meet."

"Good. I thought you were afraid of publicity," he said with a quick look.

"Not really afraid," she laughed. "Can't you just see

the gossip columns tomorrow? 'John Tabor was seen in a prominent dinner club dancing and carousing with a mystery woman.'"

Enjoying the sound of her laughter he joined the fun. "How about it, fellow carouser, do you feel like a little Texas two step?"

"I'm game if you are."

"I'll enjoy getting out of this tie and jacket. Nashville in the summer is no place for a suit."

Leaving her wrap in the car with Jake's jacket and tie, she eyed him critically.

"What's wrong?" He asked puzzled.

"You don't look ready for a 'Honky Tonk'. Here let me help," she removed his cuff links and rolled his sleeves up to his elbows, while he unbuttoned the top of his shirt.

"Ah, that's better," he sighed. "Now it's my turn," he turned her around and started fishing pins out of her hair ignoring her protests, "Ah, much better," he laughed as he tousled her curls.

"Hey," she ducked. Running her fingers through her hair to find the remaining pins, she tried to bring some semblance of order to her wild curls.

"Don't worry, it looks great," Jake grinned as he led her to the door.

A country band was playing at one end of the room,

while a group of people line danced.

Ordering soft drinks Jake asked if she'd like to join them.

"Not yet, it's been years since I line danced. I'd like to watch awhile."

When the music changed Jake led her to the floor. Taking her hand he put his arm around her, and they were off. In no time they were swing dancing around the floor.

They danced for over an hour when, much to the delight of the crowd, someone recognized Jake and before long they were clamoring for him to sing. With encouragement from Emma he consented to sing just one. Everyone gathered around the stage as Jake sang clapping and singing with him. When he finished the applause was thunderous. Calming the crowd he sang a popular hymn. The people raised their voices with his, and when the last note died away the band went into a slow tune. Couples turned and danced slowly away.

Jake placed a hand at Emma's waist and led her to the table. "Are you ready to go," he asked in a quiet voice.

Emma nodded and they turned to leave coming face to face with a sandy haired man.

"Mr. Tabor? I'm Tom Crowley a freelance photographer, would you mind if I took your picture?" The question was asked politely. Jake looked at Emma who gave an almost imperceptible nod. He put his arm around her and they smiled. The flash, although expected, startled Emma and she turned her head. Then raising laughing eyes to Jake there was another flash. The photographer gave them his business card and thanked them.

"Thank you," Jake smiled. "It's nice to be asked for a change."

"I like to treat people the way I'd like to be treated. I'm just starting out and I want to do it right." Excusing himself he left them to their privacy.

"We'll have to remember him." Jake thoughtfully fingered the card, which was emblazoned with a fish symbol used by many Christians. Then he stowed it safely in his pocket.

Chapter 10

The Sunday papers were full of pictures and speculation about her identity. Coming with the news of a new album, and a single with Jeri Forester there were many unanswered questions.

Jake and Emma at the small church he had been attending while in town were blissfully unaware of the media circus surrounding them.

Upon returning to the hotel they were pounced upon by reporters waiting at the door. Jake keeping a firm hold on Emma consented to a brief interview and took a few questions.

"John, we're happy to see you back in town. Is it true you working on a new album?"

"Yes, the new album is called 'Tangled Hearts'. The title track is being released immediately."

"Who is this lovely lady with you?"

"A friend," Jake kept a grip on her hand.

"Will there be wedding bells in the future?" A woman reporter asked archly.

"I'm not a gypsy fortune teller," he laughed, "but,

thanks for your interest folks. If I have any more news I'll call you."

With a genial wave he turned and ushered Emma into the hotel amidst a barrage of questions. The concierge rushed forward apologizing profusely. "I am sorry sir we had to put them out, they were bothering the customers."

"It's alright Antonio, I understand. Glancing at Emma he took in her flushed face. Her color was a little too high and her eyes were fever bright. She'd been quiet all day and her hand felt quite warm to his touch. Instinctively he put his hand on her forehead.

"You're burning up." His face was filled with concern as turning to Antonio he asked. "Would you send the house doctor up to our suite?"

With a nod he assured him, "yes sir, Mr. Peterson I'll send Dr. Parker, right up."

Wrapping an arm around Emma Jake hustled her to the elevator. Once in the Penthouse he led Emma to her room.

"Let's get you to bed." He left her sitting in a chair and rummaged around in the dresser.

"I'll be okay, it's only a headache, and I just need some more aspirin." She looked up at him with pain shining in her fever bright eyes.

Finding her nightgown he eyed her concerned. "Can you get changed alone?"

Nodding her head she winced. "I'll be fine," she assured him thickly.

"I'll be right outside the door, call if you need me." He stepped out and closed the door behind him.

Emma's fingers fumbled with the buttons on her blouse. Her eyes burned and she was dizzy. She felt dreadful and she wondered dully how she could have come down with something so quickly.

There was something wrong with her nightgown; she couldn't seem to get her head to go in. Finally finding the neck opening she was struggling with the sleeves, when she decided to stand. Perhaps if she straightened the fabric a bit-

Jake heard her fall and hurried into the room where he gently helped her sit up. Kneeling beside her he somehow managed to find the right places to put her arms then he scooped her up without protest and tucked her into bed. At this point she was too weary to argue with him, all she wanted to do was sleep.

When the Doctor knocked on the door, Jake was ready for him. Ushering him into her room he stepped to the other side of the bed.

"How long has she been like this?" Dr Parker asked as he felt her head and reached for a thermometer.

"I don't think she's felt well all day, she's been quiet and spoke of taking more aspirin awhile ago."

"I'm still alive here." Emma spoke, as she looked at

them with glazed eyes.

"So you are, young lady," the doctor grinned. "If you will step into the other room young man, I'll see what is going on."

Jake was pacing when Dr. Parker finally came out and closed the door.

"How is she?"

"This may not be an easy night. She has a particularly nasty flu bug. It comes on quickly and is over just as fast, but it will leave her quite weak for a while. I've given her something to help her rest and bring down her fever. Would you like me to send a nurse to stay with her?"

Jake declined the help, so handing him a bottle of pills he told him to give her two more when she awakened. Giving instructions on what to do if the fever climbed too high he told him, "the fever should break by morning, but, if it doesn't, or if you need me, don't hesitate to call me at this number." He handed him his card and took his leave.

Jake went to her room and stood watching Emma sleep. Gently he picked up her hand and falling to his knees, began to pray.

Starting awake. Jake rubbed the back of his neck and blinked. In the light from the bedside lamp he saw Emma moving restlessly and moaning. Quickly rising he tried to get her to swallow the pills the Doctor had left. Cradling her head and shoulders he finally got the medication into her. Her eyes opened and she mumbled something unintelligible. She was burning with fever, and he knew her temperature must come down at once. In the bathroom he found a basin and some towels. Wringing the towels in cool water he placed them on her face and neck.

Moaning Emma threw her arms up and mumbled something that sounded like 'no'. She began to fight him crying out, "No, no leave me alone!"

Jake tried to reassure her, "Emma, It's okay sweetheart, it's me Jake." As he tried to pull her into his arms she struggled, pushing against him in panic.

"No Carl, don't touch me!" In shock, he released her as she cried out, "Leave me alone! Don't hurt me, Oh God help me," she begged. "Please help me!" She mumbled awhile longer, as he changed her towels.

Tears ran down his face as he worked on her. When she wasn't raving about Carl she was crying and begging Doc to save Angel. At one point she grabbed his shirt and cried, "Doc, it's not Angels fault, it's not her fault, save her, let me die. Why did you bring me back? You should have left me dead." He held her in his arms as she sobbed and prayed that God would bring her safely through the sickness that racked her frail body.

After awhile she whimpered, "Jake, make the music stop," she held her head. "Make it stop. Oh Jake, where are you?" Sobbing she clung to him. "Help me Jake, don't let him touch me, please keep me safe."

He lay beside her on the bed holding her as she cried. "I'm here," he soothed. "I'm here; I'll take care of you. I won't let him touch you again, my darling."

Holding her, he continued to bathe her with the wet towels until the fever broke and exhausted; she slept deeply in his arms. He held her, his face wet with tears, crying for the pain she had been through. His love for her overflowed and he prayed that she would never again know such deep sorrow. Finally, he too slept.

The morning sun was peeking through the drapes. She stirred in his arms, wondering where she was. He gathered her closer and sleepily made soothing noises, then became still once more. Carefully she lifted her heavy head and looked with wonder at his tired face. Even though she still felt ill, she loved the way she felt as he held her. She watched him in the morning light and enjoyed the sensation of waking in his arms.

What had happened? The last thing she remembered was the Doctor giving her some pills and telling her to sleep, she felt better, but still had a terrible headache. Why was Jake in her bed holding her like he would never let her go, and looking wearier then she'd ever seen him?

In this light she could see a few threads of silver in his curly dark hair. The lines between his nose and mouth were more pronounced and there was tiredness around his eyes. She longed to smooth her hand over his forehead. Something stirred deep within her as she gazed upon him and knew without a doubt that she loved him.

Emma Winters had done the impossible she was completely and irrevocably in love. Drawing a deep shaky breath she gently ran her fingertips down his raspy cheek. His eyes opened and she was drawn into the depths of his sleepy gaze. Tightening his arms around her, his lips sought hers in a sweet kiss. Her arm crept around his shoulders as she kissed him back. Slowly he pulled back and looked into her dazed eyes. Recognition sharpened his focus and startled, he released her and scrambled off the bed. "I'm sorry, are you okay?" Running his hands through his hair he stumbled to a chair.

Not sure what she'd done wrong she shivered from the sudden loss of his body heat. Emma frowned as she realized that her gown was damp. Clearing her throat, she croaked, "What happened?"

"You had a high fever; the Doctor said it was the flu."

"Why am I wet?" she asked puzzled.

"Your fever was so high I had to keep wet towels on you. How do you feel?" He nervously watched her, not knowing if she remembered anything of the previous night.

"Like I've been dragged through a knothole

backward," she grinned. Seeing the concern on his face she told him, "I have a headache and I feel weak as a kitten. You brought my fever down with wet towels? Thank-you."

"You need to put on something dry, but I don't think I should leave you alone."

Collecting her clean gown and a spare pair of underwear, he helped her to sit up. Pulling her arms inside her gown he helped her reach out from under the hem and thread her arms into the fresh gown. Lifting the damp garment over her head she quickly slid the clean one on.

"There that wasn't too bad was it?" he asked as he gathered her and her things into his arms and carried her into the bathroom.

Overriding her protests, he reminded her of her fall the night before. He set her on her feet and made sure she was all right before he left her to her privacy.

He placed a few calls before returning to the bathroom door to check on her.

While he waited he wondered how he could have let himself kiss her like that. Waking with her in his arms, he was still half asleep when he saw the bemused look in her eyes and- no, he mustn't think how sweet she had looked, he mustn't think how she had felt in his arms. With a groan he tried to rein in his runaway thoughts.

"Father please help me in my weakness," he prayed.

He was waiting, composed, when she emerged. Once again he lifted her and carried her into the sitting room. Laying her on the sofa he covered her with a blanket tucking pillows behind her until he was satisfied that she was comfortable.

"Your shirt is wet, you should change before you get sick too," she fretted. "And I can walk. You make me feel like an invalid."

"It's high time someone took care of you. I'm not surprised you got the flu." He chastised her. "You're nothing but skin and bones and you take care of everyone but yourself."

As she opened her mouth to protest there was a knock at the door.

Jake opened to room service. He had them place a table near her so she needn't get up. Passing her a plate of food he said simply, "eat".

"Yes sir," she said with mock humility.

"That's better," he chuckled.

Housekeeping sent the maid he had requested to change her bed and bring fresh towels. Soon Dr Palmer stopped in to check on his patient. While he sent Jake to take a shower and change the Doctor examined Emma and gave her something for her headache. Then he helped her to bed where he declared her on the mend and urged her to rest. Returning to the sitting room he met Jake returning from his shower.

The Doctor eyed him critically taking in the dark circles beneath his eyes. "Rough night?"

Jake nodded. "Her fever was pretty high. I kept wet towels on her until it broke about four o'clock this morning."

"You should have called. Did you have any problem with delirium?"

"For awhile." Memories of the long night caused him to pale and grow sober.

"Apparently she's been pushing herself for a long time." The Doctor asked, "Is she a model or an actress?"

"Neither, why?"

"She's quite thin, and I'm afraid she has let herself run down. Have you known her long?"

"A few months."

The Doctor looked hard at Him. Nodding his head he smiled, he was satisfied with what he saw.

"I can see that she's pretty important to you," he spoke gently. "And I know you'll take good care of her. Make sure she gets lots of rest and regular meals and she'll be the picture of health in no time."

"Now you get some rest, Mr. Peterson, she'll sleep most of the day, and we need to keep you well. I don't think she could handle taking care of you yet and I'm afraid Antonio would have my job if I let the big boss get sick while staying here," he chuckled.

"Don't worry about Antonio. I'm grateful for your help. Thanks again." As he let the doctor out, he thanked God again for his inheritance and for the board of directors that made it possible for him to live without having to constantly be at the beck and call of the Hotel.

Jake went to stand over Emma's bed. He watched her awhile then he gently kissed her brow and said a prayer.

Not wanting to leave her alone, he investigated the love seat near her bed. Finding it to be a hide-a-bed he pulled it out and settled his long frame on the inadequate mattress and tried to sleep. Loving her was going to be the death of him. After a very long prayer he fell asleep.

The phone was ringing. Jake jumped out of bed and tripped on the blanket. Falling across Emma's empty bed, he regained his feet and staggered into the living room in time to see Emma, showered, dressed and seated on the sofa, pick up the receiver.

Smiling she motioned him over as she spoke into the mouthpiece. "Hello, oh hi Sue. No, I'm afraid I've had the flu, I haven't had the TV on." Using the remote control, she turned the television on. "What channel? Don't forget the time change." Flipping through the channels she came across a popular tabloid show. "

"I found it, okay, thanks for calling."

As they watched, the host of the program gave details of Jake and Emma's night on the town.

"After a two year hiatus John Tabor was seen this weekend dining and dancing in a Nashville dinner club with this lovely woman." There was video of them dancing at the dinner club, and footage of them line dancing. "They even had time to drop in for some line dancing at a local country music club where John gave an impromptu concert."

"John is very closemouthed about the lovely woman seen here with him outside their hotel. Whoever she is he seems to be very protective of her." They showed the interview with a close up of Jake holding her hand, and placing a protective arm around her as he led her through the hotel door.

The host summed up her report. "Two years after the death of his wife and child, John Tabor is back with a new album soon to hit stores, a great new single with the mystery songwriter Jeri Forester, and a beautiful woman on his arm. John, we here at Star Talk, wish you all the very best."

As they moved on to the next story, Emma switched off the set.

"We've been found out," she grinned. "How did they get all that footage?"

"Hidden cameras I'm sure. I wouldn't put it past

Mike Mason to do something like this he must have followed us. Are you okay?" He asked concerned over the report.

"I'm still pretty weak, but I'm felling better and I can't wait to get back to the ranch," she smiled.

"I'm glad to hear that," he said soberly. "But I'm talking about the TV coverage. I'm afraid it's a lot more than you bargained for."

Emma considered his words. "Yes, there is a lot more to this than I first thought, but I guess we can think of it as free advertising. Joe and Sue can use all the revenue they can get," she grinned, "Not to mention you. Your album is wonderful, it's just the right mixture of country and gospel it won't put anyone off and they'll still get the message."

Picking up the menu she changed the subject. "Aren't you hungry? I'm starved."

He laughed as he got to his feet. "You must be feeling better. Why don't you order this time? Just so long as we don't have to cook."

"No fondue?" She teased.

"And nothing raw," he reminded her with a laugh as he headed to his room.

"Sushi's out, I guess it'll have to be steak," she joined his laughter.

Cleaning up, and changing into comfortable jeans, he marveled at Emma's resiliency. Last night she could hardly walk and now here she was looking beautiful and worrying about feeding him. There were dark circles under her eyes that added to the air of fragility that surrounded her. He shook his head as he thought about last night. It was apparent she had been attacked at some point in her life. And who was Angel? There were so many unanswered questions.

He thought about how he had planned to declare his love for her and ask her to marry him while they were out dancing. The time hadn't been right, and now having seen the broadcast, he understood why the ring was still in his suit pocket.

Looking in the mirror he asked himself if the startling revelations of the last night had changed how he felt. The answer was a definite yes. Now he wanted nothing more than the opportunity to protect and shield her from all the unpleasant things in life. Knowing some of the hardships she'd endured made him respect and admire her even more. The tasteful way she dealt with the press, while retaining her ladylike stature was remarkable. Her wit and often-dry humor got her through some pretty rough situations. Since she'd given her heart and life to God she had grown both spiritually and emotionally.

There was a knock at his door.

"Supper's ready." she called.

"I'm coming," he said as he opened the door.

Supper was a happy time though she could only eat about half of the petite portion she'd ordered. As they laughed and joked he watched her carefully. When she seemed to be drooping a little, he insisted she get ready for bed.

"Only if I can come back out. I'm tired but, not sleepy, please..." She whined deliberately adding a sad puppy look with a pout.

"Just this once," he teased sternly.

"Thanks Dad," she said dryly. "Um, there's one other thing," she reddened. "Could I borrow a T shirt? My night gowns are, well-"

"Sure," he broke in, "need anything else?"

"No, that's all."

He brought her a huge navy blue shirt, and she retired to change into it and shorts.

When she returned, the dishes were gone.

"Could we take room service home with us?" She asked. "Just for the dishes?"

"Hey, I like doing dishes with you," he laughed; as they sat on the couch she tucked her feet under her. Eyeing her he commented. "You look about fourteen in that outfit."

"Thanks, you're good for my self esteem," she grinned. "Anything good on TV?"

Finding a movie they both liked they settled in to watch it. About halfway through, Emma caught a chill and started shivering. Reaching for the blanket at the same time they collided and losing her balance she fell off the couch. He tried to catch her and she went down pulling him on top of her. Laughing and shivering they finally made it back onto the couch with the blanket.

Jake pulled her into his arms wrapped her in the blanket and held her close until she stopped shivering. Warm and drowsy she enjoyed just being held by him a weakness that was not associated with her illness stole over her limbs as she murmured, "I could stay right here forever."

His arms tightened around her and she realized she had spoken aloud. Lifting her eyes she gazed at him as he smoothed the hair from her forehead and brushed a feather light kiss at her hairline. He saw the dawning light in her eyes as they begged him for more. Her lips parted as she caught her breath at what she saw in his face. With gentleness he didn't know he possessed, he kissed her. The blood pounded in his temples as he fought for control. Resting her head in the hollow of his shoulder, he held her trembling form until their breathing quieted.

"We can't do this," he sighed into her hair. "I feel like I'm going crazy."

"You aren't the only one." She drew a shaky breath. "Why do you make me feel this way?"

"Does it frighten you?"

She nodded her head thoughtfully. "A little."

"Emma I don't want to frighten you," he said seriously. "You know I'd never hurt you, but we're only human. We need to stay out of situations like this.

"I'm sorry, I should go to bed," she said coloring as she disentangled herself.

He stood and without warning scooped her up.

As her arms went around his neck she protested. "Jake, I can walk."

"I know, but you won't usually let anyone help you, so I'm taking advantage of this."

"Oh, well, in that case 'carry on'," she laughed as he dumped her in the bed.

"Don't tease me, young lady, or I'll take my shirt back!" She laughed at his silliness as he tucked her into bed

Taking her hand they prayed together. When they finished he ran a hand over her curls.

"Go to sleep," he commanded gently.

"Yes sir," she demurred.

"It's too bad you aren't always this obedient," he chuckled as she made a face at him.

Smiling, he closed her door. Purposely he walked across the room and entering his bedroom firmly closed the door behind him. Not knowing how he would survive another day in this suite alone with her, he dropped to his knees beside the bed.

Chapter 11

The evening sun made long shadows on the road before them. They had been driving the back roads around Nashville and enjoying the parts of town tourists normally didn't see.

After Dr. Palmer had examined Emma that morning, Jake suggested an afternoon drive. It was good to get out. Neither of them was used to being cooped up indoors.

Emma stretched lazily in the passenger seat of the car.

"Tired?" Jake asked.

"No, it's been a heavenly day," she smiled. "I almost forgot what inactivity felt like."

"After the way you've worked these past months, I can see why you are worn out." He shot her a serious look. "Dr. Palmer wanted to know why you are so run down. I couldn't tell him, because I didn't know."

"I was unwell for quite a long while. I'm afraid I didn't really care what happened to me."

She had that closed look about her again and even

though Jake wanted to question her, he held back. When the time was right she would open up about it herself.

"Well, I'm glad you're doing better. All this driving is making me hungry. How does this place look?" The roadside cafe ahead bore a large sign advertising, "The Best Ribs in Town"

Laughing, she accused, "You are trying to fatten me up!"

"I feel like barbecued ribs." He laughed with her.

"That's strange, you don't look like barbecued ribs," She teased.

Laughing and joking they enjoyed a delicious meal of ribs, French fries, coleslaw and baked beans.

Declaring she couldn't eat another bite, Emma leaned back in the booth and sighed. "This has been a wonderful day." Sipping her coffee, she asked, "what time do we have to be at the airport in the morning?"

"Eight o'clock. We should leave the hotel at seven, if that's not too early."

"Seven too early?" she grinned. "I'm usually in the middle of making breakfast by seven."

"It will be good to get back to the ranch. I've never been a big fan of city life."

"Sue mentioned you had my cabin built before you

were married. Where did you and Amy live?"

"In the Denver area, we actually had a house out in Aurora. After the accident I didn't care about anything anymore. Joe and Sue asked me to come back to the ranch, so I put the house on the market and walked out on everything." He sighed there was a faraway look in his eyes.

"When I got back someone else was using the cabin. I didn't need the sound proofing because I had quit singing, so I moved into the cabin next to it." Looking into her eyes he said, "I'm glad you have it, you appreciate the qualities built into it."

"Won't you need it again, now that you've resumed working?" Emma asked curiously.

"Occasionally, if you don't mind, I may borrow your studio," he smiled.

"I don't mind at all," she smiled back. "I've ordered some new equipment you may like." Filling him on her new acquisition they gathered their things to leave.

When they stopped at the cash register to pay their bill the waitress shyly held out a piece of paper and asked Jake for his autograph. Smiling, Jake wrote, 'Thanks for the delicious ribs, John Tabor'.

Amidst profuse thanks, they took their leave and were soon on their way.

"Some day you'll be the one signing autographs, and I'll be the one watching. Just don't forget which name to use." As she chuckled, he continued, "I signed one Jake Peterson once, the young girl looked at it and said, 'Oh, I'm sorry. I thought you were John Tabor.' and walked away. I didn't have the heart to tell her the truth." Amidst peals of laughter he continued. "You can be sure that didn't happen again."

At her urging he had her laughing at his amusing anecdotes. He asked her about her work in the clubs, and she told him her amusing stories. They arrived at the hotel tired, but in high spirits.

*   *   *

Turning off the highway, Emma remembered the first time she'd traveled this road. It had been mid April, and wild flowers had dotted the landscape. Now it was October, The aspen trees were a lovely golden mass on the hillside with bright red oaks interspersed among them. She was glad to be home.

Home, was the ranch her home? How much longer would she be able to stay there? The answer was easy, she would stay as long as she was needed and Jake wanted her there.

Jake had been careful not to get too close the last few days and she burned with embarrassment as she remembered the way she had practically thrown herself at him that night in the hotel. The trip on the airplane was uneventful, and they'd checked into a motel near the airport in Denver. Jake had told her he needed to take care of some business in the city. She had remained at the motel rather than go shopping, and this morning they had gotten under way early. They should be at the ranch by lunchtime.

"I hope Penny is working out alright. I'm glad she was available to help out with so little notice."

Jake glanced at her, "Are you worried she'll replace you?"

Emma looked serious. "When Doc first approached me about coming out here, he said Joe and Sue needed help while Sue was laid up." She was silent for a moment. "I guess I am worried, a little. I've come to love the ranch, and the kids are precious. I haven't felt so safe, and needed in years."

Safe. The word jumped out at Jake reminding him of her cries the other night. He wanted to pull the car over and beg her to stay, not as an employee, but as his wife, but he knew that he needed to wait until she had worked through the trauma that she had been through. Containing his impatience he would keep to his plan.

"You are needed at the ranch. Sue can't handle everything herself, with the baby coming, not to mention the renovations soon to begin. While I was in Denver I checked on the trust account." He named the sizeable amount already deposited by the record company." Taking hold of her hand he said, "You can't leave yet. We need you." And his heart cried out, 'I need you.'

Emma's world became bright once more and her

smile reflected it.

The final strains of 'Tangled Hearts' were wafting from the radio on the kitchen windowsill. Penny and Sue stood in rapt attention; they turned tear bright eyes toward the door as Emma walked in.

"Oh Em!" Sue cried, as she hurried across the room and threw her arms around Emma, "I love it."

Penny who had been entrusted with who Emma's secret joined in the praise. "How did you ever get it so perfect?"

"We didn't. We just prayed and God did the rest." Emma was touched by their reaction.

"Thanks for keeping my secret Penny. There are very few people who know who I am."

"I'm honored you would trust me." Penny smiled. "Thank you."

Sue was watching her friends closely. She had confided to Penny that she hoped Emma and Jake would have some good news when they returned home. Emma didn't look like a prospective bride and there was no ring on her finger.

"Are you okay Em. You look pale."

"I'm fine now, I had the flu while we were in Nashville, but I'm ready to go back to work."

"Oh no you're not." Jake objected as he walked in the door. "Dr Palmer said you are to take a few more days off."

Emma whirled around at the sound of his voice. "I'll be fine. I can't just hang around and do nothing." She protested with a trace of impatience.

"You'll be plenty busy. Helping with the kids isn't too strenuous. Penny's here to help with the kitchen work, and," his lips twitched and his eyes sparkled with humor, "you won't have to cook."

Suddenly she was smiling all bad humor gone. "No fondue?" she asked.

"And no sushi." They recited in unison, laughing at the confusion of their audience.

Sue looked from Jake to Emma with a smile and stopped worrying. Everything would work out just fine.

Penny sent Sue a confused glance. "I've never made Fondue or sushi."

Joe walked in on the ensuing laughter.

"What's so funny?" He asked as he greeted Jake and gave Emma a bear hug.

Emma tried to explain as the 'boys' erupted into the room, then gave up in the excitement that followed.

Over lunch, Jake and Emma took some good-natured ribbing over their media coverage.

"I sure wish I'd known you could line dance like

that Miss Emma." Slim declared. "Jenny's been trying to get me to learn. But I got two left feet."

"Romeo's good at it," Penny chimed in. "Why don't you bring Jenny to the dance in town on Friday night?"

Romeo seconded the invitation. He was clearly smitten with the lively redhead.

Emma smiled; glad things were working out for them.

*   *   *

Joe faced Jake across the office desk. "I can't let you keep doing this Jake."

"It wasn't entirely my fault this time," Jake raised his hands in protest. "Em had her half of the proceeds from 'Tangled Hearts' set up before she left for Nashville."

"I know, she told us, but that's not what I'm talking about and you know it." With a sigh he handed his brother-in-law the deed to the ranch. "This came while you were gone. The ranch has been paying for itself and we've been making regular payments on what we owe you." He stated. "When you kept us from loosing this place it was with the understanding that we would pay you back."

"You've done that and more. I can't begin to tell you what it's meant for me to be here. After Amy and Candy died I was a wreck. You may not know it, but I came very close to ending my own life. The media wouldn't leave me alone and I just couldn't take anymore. Then you and Susie came through for me, you gave me a place to go and something to work for." He looked seriously at his friend.

"I was just as handicapped as those kids, and you treated me just as well. Your support and prayers have been more payment than I could have asked for."

"When you married my sister, you made her happier than I've ever seen her. It wasn't our parent's intention to cause a hardship on you by tying her inheritance up till she was twenty-seven. I'm sure it seemed a good idea at the time, she was running around with a bad crowd, and they were worried. I know Mom and Dad would have approved of you."

"Your mother did the right thing mortgaging the ranch to pay for your father's cancer treatments."

There was pain in Joe's eyes as he said, "I wish we could have saved Dad, we tried everything and when he was gone Mom didn't have anything left to live for. I hope you realize that I would never use Sue's inheritance to fund the ranch." Joe hated having to lean on anyone. He was fiercely independent. "I didn't even want you to know we were in trouble."

"If Sue hadn't come to me asking if the will could be broken I never would have guessed. I was too wrapped up in my own misery to notice things weren't right and you would have lost the ranch.

Helping you get this place in working order again gave me something to live for.

"We still can't let you give us the deed to the ranch. It isn't right."

"Call it a gift for your baby's future. I want this little one to have a place he can be proud of. Something he can pass on to his children." Jake smiled. "Besides when Sue comes into her inheritance next year, you will be taking a load off my shoulders."

"Have you told Emma that you own Hancock Hotels?" Joe asked.

"No, and I'd like to keep it quiet a while longer." Jake sobered. "I don't think she's ready for that revelation. "I want her to be fully recuperated both physically and spiritually before I ask her to marry me. The flu really took it out of her and she needs time to recuperate."

Seeing the remembered fear in Jake's eyes Joe rushed to speak. "Emma Winters is stronger then you realize. Remember that day she almost passed out?" At Jake's nod he continued, "I called Doc Linden that afternoon and told him what was going on. I wanted to know the score so I'd know what to expect. Doc couldn't say much 'patient confidentiality' he called it. But it seems something happened about five years ago that set her back for awhile. Every time she started getting over it she got hit with another blow. I guess she finally just cut herself off from everyone and all emotions, afraid of being hurt again."

Smiling he continued, "When she got saved, it was a blessed miracle. The dam broke on all the pain and bitterness she had held inside for so long, but 'Tangled Hearts' has shown me that she still has a lot of issues she needs to deal with. I think you're wise to wait on future plans until she has her feet firmly under her."

"Thanks Joe, I appreciate the explanation and the concern you've shown. I wish this whole Jeri Forester thing could have been left on the shelf for a time, but the more I prayed about it, the more I was sure it was time for it to come forth. God will use it for his glory, I'm certain of it." He heaved a heavy sigh. "Just pray for me, I'm not the world's most patient man and I need Gods strength to do things in His time."

Joe assured him with a grin that he would pray. He knew that Sue wasn't the only Peterson who had been a bit wild in their youth.

*   *   *

The early morning air had a bite to it. Emma's heart was singing as she walked to the kitchen. Jake had finally relented and let her come back to work. Providing Penny stayed and helped the first day. She didn't like not being busy it left her too much time to think.

She had been active riding fences with Jake looking for places that needed fixing. She had gone with

Sue on supply runs, and helped her with errands, but running errands didn't make her feel needed. Jake had been friendly but had kept his distance from her. Sometimes she wondered if she had dreamed the intimate closeness that they had shared in Nashville.

The arrival of the new equipment she'd ordered had helped some, but the long nights still stretched ahead of her. Refusing to allow herself the memory of waking in Jake's arms, she had kept a firm hold on her imagination.

If only she could control her dreams. No more were her nights filled with fear. Now she dreaded the sweet dreams of being with Jake with all the barriers down. Not just the friendship he had offered this past week, but a deeper richer relationship, an intimacy of body and soul that she only wanted to share in the bonds of matrimony. Her thoughts made her blush; she had been shocked that she could think such thoughts

Emma knew she had never committed her relationship with Jake to God. She struggled with the knowledge that if she wanted true fulfillment in all aspects of her life that God was the only one who could bring it about.

For years she had neatly placed her life into certain categories carefully filing them into an emotional void. Lately God had a habit of pulling a file and upsetting the delicate balance of her system. Just when she had integrated one file into the rest of her life, she'd discovered another ready to be dealt with.

The strain had carried over into her songwriting, she'd struggled with a particular tune last night, until frustrated, she'd cried out to God for help. After pouring out her frustrations and committing her life, all her life, to Him again, she'd picked up her bible and flipped it open. It opened to Psalm twenty-seven and her eyes fell on the fifth verse. She began to read.

'For in the time of trouble he shall hide me in his pavilion: in the secret of his tabernacle shall he hide me; he shall set me up upon a rock.'

Incredibly, the tune in her head straightened out and words began to flow.

"There is a place where I can go, when troubles come and cold winds blow.

A place of rest, a place of peace, a place where I find Victory.

Where I leave my past behind, and finally find true peace of mind.

It's where Gods word has said to go it's His pavilion in my soul.

With Gods help, Emma had dropped into a deep peaceful sleep that night knowing that whatever troubles came her way she could handle anything with Him on her side.

Chapter 12

Things had, once again, settled into a routine. Emma made breakfast each morning, while Sue slept in. She was six months along and Emma kept a protective watch over her. The baby was growing and everything seemed to be progressing normally.

Sometimes Sue chaffed over the watchful eyes of everyone at the ranch. Today was no exception.

Joe was hovering over her as she watched Jake and Emma finish cleaning the kitchen.

"We need to be on the road by ten-thirty to make your doctors appointment on time," he told her.

"I'm so tired of going to the Doctor. First with my ankle and now the baby, I'm sick of doctor's offices. I don't think it will hurt to miss one little appointment," she wheedled.

With her back to them they didn't notice that Emma had stopped wiping the counter. She stood stock still, tension building within her at a fever pitch as the blood drained from her face.

"Come on honey you know they want to monitor your progress." Joe grinned.

Sue was out of sorts and didn't feel like being submissive. With a stubborn look she announced, "Joseph Andrew Jacobs, women have been having babies for thousands of years without all this fuss. Everything's just fine, I would know if it wasn't."

"NO!" The sound had erupted from Emma who turning had a look of terror on her sickly white face. "Don't say that! You can't know- you can't know if something's wrong!"

Hurrying to the table she planted her hands on its firm surface and leaned toward Sue. "You think you have everything under control then, your life falls apart and you lose everything precious to you." Tears filled her eyes. "You lose everything."

Her despair was so complete that she failed to notice when Jake gently urged her into a chair.

"Emma?" Sue gently voiced the question that had been burning in everyone's minds for months. "What happened honey?"

Slowly Emma focused tortured eyes on her friend's face. "It's time, I can't keep it in anymore, and you have to know the truth. I've wanted to tell you, but I was so afraid." For the past few months she had avoided the inevitable. She had known the time would come when she would tell them the whole story and now she wanted to get it over with. Taking a deep breath she clutched her hands to her heart and lowered her eyes on the table as in a tortured voice she started from the beginning.

"I had a country band in college. Six months before graduation we played at a party in downtown Denver. I was the last of the band members to leave. When my car wouldn't start I-I was so stupid; I let this man from the party drive me home." Burying her face in her hands she continued embarrassed. "I didn't realize he'd had so much to drink. He made an excuse and I let him in my apartment, "her voice broke from the strain the memories placed on her fragile control and she shook as if she had a chill. "I was so naive. I never thought he would hurt me, but he was drunk, and people do things when they're drunk they wouldn't normally do, and he, he..." Her control snapped and the tears ran through her fingers falling heedless to the tabletop.

Sue watching horrified said quietly, "He forced himself on you. Oh honey, I'm sorry but it wasn't your fault. That's why you were so worried about Penny. What did the police say?"

Emma shook her head, her breath catching in the throat. "I-I didn't tell them. I didn't tell anyone. I-I couldn't face anyone. I couldn't stand to be on stage again. I felt like everyone could see what had happened. The band didn't understand why I quit. I told them my grades were suffering, but they didn't believe me. I was too ashamed to tell anyone the truth." Emma's face was as pale as a moonstone as she looked at Sue. Taking a shaky breath she continued.

"It was a couple of months before I realized I was pregnant."

Sue gasped. Emma wouldn't look at Jake; she focused on Joe and Sue. "At first I was devastated. I didn't want his baby, but abortion was out of the question. Then one day I felt her move and I knew she was mine." Sue reached for her hand and held tight. "Don't ask me how I knew she was a girl. I guess I had a fifty-fifty chance of being right."

Jake's voice broke into her thoughts. "You called her Angel." She turned to him a question frozen on her lips by the look in his eyes. "When you were sick you called for her."

"Oh Jake I'm sorry, no wonder you were so tired the next day."

Jake raised her hand to his lips and placing a kiss on her fingers he said, "I'm glad I was there for you."

Emma, feeling the support of the man she loved she looked into his eyes and continued. "'Daddy's Girl' was a hard song for me to send off. You see I wanted it to be more personal, but that's the way it came and I couldn't change it, so I secretly called it 'Mommy's girl'. I didn't want anyone to know my secret."

Turning to Sue she confided. "The morning sickness was constant. My friends thought I was bulimic so I cut myself off from everyone. Then when I went to graduation Doc saw me, and he knew. He asked me to go to lunch with him the next day. I showed up in my big sweater and waited for him in his office as usual."

"When he came in he told me he could tell I was pregnant, he asked how far along I was and who my doctor was. I broke down and told him the whole story" Tears started down her cheeks again. "He said the baby wasn't big enough for six months, and did an ultra sound. He saw a problem with Angel's heart and he was worried. He called Dr Hanson's office and drove me over there that same day."

"They put me in the hospital right away and the next morning took me to surgery. You see there was a chance Dr Hanson could fix the problem while Angel was still inside of me." As she told of the surgery and death of Angel she broke into sobs.

Jake looked as though his heart was being torn in two as he held her letting her cry. Then even though he knew it was tearing her apart he encouraged her to continue. He instinctively knew that she must let all the bitterness out if she were to start healing.

Sue cried softly as she clung to Joe.

After awhile Emma dried her eyes took a deep breath and continued her story. "Even after Angel was gone my-my body thought it was still pregnant, I kept throwing everything up and I got so thin I had to be hospitalized again. They gave me intravenous hormones because I couldn't keep anything down. My body was so out of balance I cried almost constantly. That's why I can't seem to gain weight. But my heart was in worse shape than my body, it had stopped on the operating table and they had a hard time bringing me around again. I wanted to die. I hated myself for what I thought was my fault. I felt I had killed Angel by not going to the doctor sooner."

Sue was stricken, "I'm so sorry Emma, and I had no idea."

"I know, some things are hard to understand. God knows I still don't understand it myself." Shaking her head she continued.

"Just when I was finally starting to heal 'Daddy's Girl' came out and the pain started all over again." At Jake's gasp she ran a hand down his cheek and pulled his arms tighter around her.

Resting her head back in the hollow of his shoulder she continued. "I couldn't eat or sleep. I had nightmares all the time. Doc feared for my sanity and put me to work cooking for the Job Corps. Hard work helped and I started coming out of the depression. Doc told me I needed to tell Angels father about the defect." Drawing a deep breath she looked at Sue and said. "You see the defect was congenital, passed on through the father, but I just couldn't. I couldn't face him I-I didn't want him to know about Angel. I didn't want him to know I had let her die"

"Almost two years after I got pregnant, just when I started to believe I'd be okay. I found out that Angel's father had gotten married and his wife was having a baby." Eyes wide she was not aware of the tortured look on everyone's faces. "I couldn't let another baby die; I couldn't let another woman go through what I'd gone through. I'd do anything to keep that from happening. I called Doc and Thank God she was one of his patients. He tested her and found the same defect, but they were able to repair her problem. It wasn't as severe. Her baby was born and is doing fine."

"Angel's father figured out what happened, by something Doc had said. He called me, but I threatened to call the police if he ever contacted me again." Straightening she pulled herself out of Jake's arms.

"I've tried to go on with my life. I even tried dating a few times, but I was afraid to be alone with another man and I always drove my own car. I just couldn't stand to let a man get near me until I found someone I could trust."

Turning to Jake, her eyes pleaded with him to understand. She held her hands out in supplication. Surely they wouldn't want her there anymore now they knew about her.

"I'm so sorry; I know I shouldn't be here. Please forgive me for not telling you before, but I'm s-so ashamed. I thought God could forgive me but, how could he?" Jumping up from her chair she ran blindly for the door.

"Emma!" Strong hands gripped her shoulders stopping her in her tracks. Burying her face in her hands she sobbed. "No, no I'm a terrible person. Angel died because of me. I killed her…"

Jake turned her around, and gripping her shoulders he shook her roughly, before pulling her into his arms. "No, that's not what happened. My darling don't, don't torture yourself please, please, listen to me. What happened to Angel wasn't your fault. It was out of your control. Hasn't being here with these children taught you any thing?"

"I was there when you gave your life to God. You didn't ask forgiveness for part of your sins and mistakes so God didn't partially forgive you. He forgave ALL your sin!"

"But…"

"No buts. God didn't say that he would forgive you for everything, except this or that. He said, everything, period! The Bible says to confess your sins one to another and well. I'd say you just did that. You aren't alone any more, Christ is in you and I'm here too. We're all here, you're a part of us now." Gently he soothed her as if she were a child. "I don't know how he'll do it but, I know God has a plan, and some day he'll use your story to help others who are hurting."

Clinging to him as if she were drowning, she slowly calmed and as the realization seeped into her consciousness that Jake and the others, didn't hate her for what had happened, she relaxed and remembered the words she had come to love from Pslam 27.

'For in the time of trouble he shall hide me in his pavilion: in the secret of his tabernacle shall he hide me; he shall set me up upon a rock.'

"Oh God, I'm sorry I didn't think you forgave me for all my past. I don't know how you can take something so painful and ugly and use it for your glory, but I'm willing to do whatever I can." She prayed with fervor.

Jake smiling prayed with her.

*   *   *

When Sue returned from Doc's office, Emma went to her sitting room to check on her friend.

"Doc said everything was just fine and he had a message for you Em. He said to tell you that this baby boy is strong like you are, so quit worrying."

It took a moment for the full import of the message to sink in. "Baby boy, it's a boy!" Emma shouted happily as she hugged Sue.

"Oh Emma, little Joe jr. is going to be just fine."

"Thank God," For the first time Emma tentatively reached a hand towards Sue's swollen abdomen.

"Go ahead little Joe's been active all afternoon." Taking Emma's hand, Sue placed it on her stomach. "Here, feel that?"

"Wow, it feels so different from this side." Emma grinned.

"I can hardly wait for you to have another one," Sue

smiled.

Emma crimsoned, "I don't think that will be happening any time soon."

"Have faith Em, you never know what God will do."

"Yeah, that sounds good, but I only have one problem."

"You aren't still afraid of intimacy are you? Sometimes when you and Jake are together I have the feeling you are walking a very fine line. I'm not sure if I should knock your heads together, or close the door and give you your privacy."

"Sue!" Emma cried shocked. Then as her friend gave her a saucy grin she sighed and confided. "It's strange; sometimes I think he may not be over Amy. I don't know why, but every time we start to get close he pushes me away. Men are so odd, they're either trying to climb all over you, or they treat you like you have leprosy and are afraid to come within touching distance."

"Don't worry Em, I know Jake loves you. I think maybe he's just afraid to push you too fast." With a thoughtful look she observed. "He said you called out for Angel when you were sick. I wonder what else you may have said."

Emma paled. "Oh no, if it was anything like my nightmares, it must have been awful. No wonder he didn't want to spend time with me in Denver, he said he had a business meeting."

"Yeah, he had a board meeting at the Hancock's main office." Sue said absently.

Confusion colored Emma's voice. "Hancock Hotels? Why would Jake go to the board meeting of a Luxury Hotel chain?"

"Uh oh," Sue gasped. "I thought you knew." As Emma shook her head Sue sighed. "Jake's going to kill me for this. I think he wants to tell you himself."

"Sue! What are you talking about?"

"My Father was owner of the Hancock Hotel chain. There are Hotels in most major cities in the States and in four foreign countries," she explained. "Since Dad's death, Jake is now the sole owner of Hancock Hotels."

Emma's mouth opened in shock and she felt the blood drain from her face. "Whoa, take it easy. Here sit down." Sue cried as she led her to a chair.

Emma's knees buckled and she sank down. "Sue this changes everything," she said weakly. "He can't want me."

"Get a grip on yourself you silly goose, of course he wants you. That's probably why he's afraid to be alone with you. What happened between you two while you were gone?"

Upon receiving a thumbnail sketch of their time

together, Sue took on a thoughtful look.

"Hmm, I'll bet the sexual tension in that suite was thick enough to cut with a knife." As Emma's face crimsoned she continued. "I'd say he's scared he can't keep his hands off you. That's why he's trying to keep you at arms length; he doesn't want you to be afraid of him."

"I'm afraid alright. I'm afraid I'll make a fool of myself. I'm afraid every time he comes into the room that I'll throw myself at him. And I'm afraid he doesn't want a crazy psychotic woman, who scared him to death that first morning by screaming the house down when I had a nightmare."

"What?"

Emma filled her in on her first meeting with Jake. "I wasn't sure how he would treat me later in the kitchen, but I was glad when he acted as if he didn't know me. I wanted to act as if I didn't know me! And oh, that black eye, my hand hurt for a week!"

Sue started laughing. "I'm sorry I know it's not something to laugh about. I just can't help but think that you've had almost as much trouble with my brother, as I had with Joe. I'd been something of a bad girl before we met at a Christian camp we both went to just out of college. Jake made me go as a counselor. I was in trouble again and he'd had come to my rescue, but this time he made me do what he called 'community service'. Well, it's a long story, but after I found the Lord I ended up here, helping with the kids. I chased Joe until he couldn't run anymore." Sue blushed profusely. "We were married after a rather stormy courtship."

As Emma broke into laughter, Sue said. "Don't laugh at me young lady what we need is a plan. Jake Peterson has interfered in my love life from the time I was fourteen years old, and now it's my turn."

Hearing a car pull up Emma said good- bye to Sue.

"Why do I feel like I'm riding a runaway train?" She wondered aloud as she went out to meet Gracie.

This was a special day for Gracie. She had done so well practicing her balance that today would be her first time riding without the harness.

Everyone available gathered at the corral for the big event. Gracie graciously waved to her audience. Then without help she mounted Sparkles her horse and carefully placed her feet clad in new red riding boots into the stirrups.

Emma placed a hand on her knee and smiling said, "Don't be nervous you know you can do this."

Gracie sat very straight and looked Emma in the eye. "I know I can," she smiled, and then her arms went around Emma in a warm hug. "I have a good teacher. Thanks for the extra help." Then she rode around the corral to the enthusiastic applause of all watching.

Emma cautiously opened the gate and Joe and Jake accompanied her on a ride along the bridle path to the river and back.

Bringing a triumphant Gracie into the corral they supervised her as she dismounted her horse. Then leading him into the stable she unsaddled and cared for him under Ken's watchful eye.

Emma remembered the thrill of her first "solo" ride with Mac, when she had been at camp so long ago. Gracie's accomplishments were so much sweeter knowing how hard she had worked to gain Joe's trust.

After Gracie finished with the horse they all went into the main Lodge for refreshments.

One by one the ranch hands congratulated the girl.

"You'd better watch out Slim or Miss Gracie's goanna get you're job." Ken teased good-naturedly.

"My job? Why this girl can care for a horse 'bout as good as you can," he teased back.

Joe and Sue once again praised Gracie as she left with her parents. Skipping happily to the car she waved good-bye as they drove away.

Emma hummed to herself as she prepared the evening meal. The song of praise on her lips that she had written earlier that day.

"When I think of All you've done for me: I praise you!

Your abiding grace has set me free!

You make me smile!"

Bowing her head she prayed for Gracie. The child had surmounted an incredible handicap and come out on top. She did it with a tenacity that would let nothing stand in the way of her goal. There was a great lesson to be learned from one so young.

Emma felt a calling in her life to minister to children and young people hurting from the pain of birth defects and handicaps, both the physical and emotional pain. She knew she needed to take an active role in prevention and researching treatments. There must be a way to raise a much greater awareness of the problem.

"Dearest Father," she prayed. "I know you have a plan for me. I've been content to sit on the sidelines for far too long. I want to do your will even if it means revealing who I am to the public to get their attention. Please lead me; I don't want anyone to get hurt by my actions. If Cindy were to figure out what happened, it might destroy her and Katie, and I don't want that to happen. I've grown to like and respect Cindy and every time I see Katie it's like watching a little bit of Angel. Help me know what to do and how to do it, in your precious name I pray, Amen."

Chapter 13

"Lord you know I want to wait on you. I know your timing is perfect. Emma needs time to heal, so I'm asking for your help to be patient. Sometimes, I'm afraid to be alone with her, I love her so much, but I don't want her frightened and I don't want to get into a compromising situation."

Another early morning after another restless night, how long could he keep this up? As he switched the coffee maker on and headed in to get dressed Jake continued to pray. Prayer was all that kept him going these days.

Gathering a clean handkerchief and picking up the odd assortment of things he kept in his pockets he paused. There were his keys and a small velvet bag with a silver cross and the key to his old cabin tied to the drawstrings. Opening the bag he removed a diamond ring. As he held it he wondered how long it would be before he felt the time was right to give it to Emma. Sighing he returned it to the bag and placed it in his pocket.

Bundling against the cold he took his coffee to the front porch. The sky was beginning to lighten. He looked toward Emma's cabin. She should be waking any time now. He resisted the urge to use his key and tiptoe into her room. The memory of waking with her in his arms was almost too much for him. She had said she was afraid to be alone with or let other men touch her, but the memory of how she had come alive in his arms made his heart pound and gave him hope. Surely she wouldn't have responded like that unless she loved and trusted him.

Placing a firm hold on his emotions he continued to pray for guidance.

*   *   *

Penny burst into the kitchen after breakfast, looking for Sue and Emma.

"Jake said I'd find you here she smiled.

"Penny what happened to you?" Sue asked taking in the radiant glow of the woman before her. "Did Romeo finally-"

"Yes!" she cried, unable to keep it in any longer. Holding out her left hand she showed her ring to them. "He asked me last night after church. He got down on one knee and everything. I'm so happy!"

Emma and Sue exclaimed over the ring and listened to all the details, thrilled over their friend's happiness.

They'd decided to wait at least six months before getting married. Penny explained that Romeo who's real name was Mark Romano had only been a Christian for two weeks and she wanted him to have time to become rooted in the faith before too many distractions came along.

"Now we just need to 'corral' Jake as Romeo puts it. I want you to be as happy as I am Emma."

Penny and Sue began once again to give Emma advice on how to make Jake take notice of her.

"Emma, how is this supposed to work if you don't cooperate?" Sue complained when she wouldn't let Sue undo another button on her blouse.

"I don't feel comfortable with my blouse unbuttoned so far and I don't think this is a good idea. I've already thrown my old t-shirts to the back of the closet and I'm trying to look more lady like, but I refuse to look…'skanky'."

"No one asked you to look 'skanky', just a little less uptight." Sue chastised her. "That's not indecent."

"I think your hormones are getting the better of you." Emma groused.

"Oh Em, when you go fishing for a man, you have to use the right bait."

Emma eyed her friend warily, in the month since she had confided her feelings to her. Sue had launched a full-fledged campaign on Jake and Emma. Everything from complementing Emma in front of Jake to sending them on errands together. Now she even had Penny in on it.

Lately the strain was beginning to show. Jake had

grown more withdrawn then ever before and Emma felt that she was near the breaking point.

"Sue this has got to stop. I want Jake to love me for the woman I am, not for some image I throw at him. What happened to having faith? I've committed my relationship with Jake into Gods hands. Quit worrying, when the time is right everything will fall into place."

"I'm sorry honey; I just can't stand seeing you two so torn up. I want you to be happy."

With a reassuring hug Emma encouraged her. "'True happiness comes to those who wait,'" she misquoted with a smile for both of them.

"Now I have to get going. I heard a car pull up and it must be Katie. They're back from vacation and she'll be raring to go." Laughing she fled from the building and headed for the stables. Leaving the two schemers behind.

Still smiling she rounded the barn, looking for Katie. What she saw had her stopping dead in her tracks, the smile frozen in place. As the blood drained from her face she stared at the man talking with Jake. Five years had changed him. There was more depth to his face. Lines were firmly drawn around his mouth and even as she watched the deep dimple flashed in his left cheek. There was quite a lot of silver in his blonde breeze ruffled hair and as he turned and looked directly at her she saw shock register across his features.

Finding her legs still under her, Emma was surprised to realize that she no longer feared him. Straightening her spine she approached.

"Hello Carl.'

Jake stiffened, recognizing the name of the man she had fought off in her delirious state. Moving to stand at Emma's side he waited.

"Emma, it is you. I saw the report on TV and the pictures in the papers. Cindy said it was you and so did Katie. I had to come. Is there someplace we can talk?"

"Over by the stable." Turning to Jake and seeing the protective look on his face, she assured him, "I'll be alright."

Leading the way she didn't go far stopping in sight of the corral where Joe was getting an enthusiastic Katie into her harness.

Jake motioned to Slim and asked him to help Joe. Slim noticed the way his eyes never wavered off the white faced Emma.

"I'm here if you need back-up." He laid his hand briefly on Jake's tense shoulder and turned toward Joe. An unspoken message flashed between the two men as Joe's eyes followed his to the couple standing by the stable.

"Why have you come?" Emma asked the pale man standing before her.

"I had to see for myself that you were alright. Cindy knows what happened. After we found out about Katie's heart, I was in Doc's office and he said we were lucky. There had been another baby with the same defect that hadn't made it, and it had nearly destroyed the mother who had been left to deal with it all alone. When I asked him who it was, he only said, 'I think you already know.' I thought he was going to kill me for a moment, But all he said was, 'May God have mercy on your soul.'"

Tears slid unheeded down his cheeks as he continued. "That phrase haunted me. I tried to call you; I wanted to tell you how sorry I was that I'd caused you so much pain. I didn't even know if the baby was a boy or a girl. Then when Katie was born I went to pieces. I told Cindy what had happened. I told her everything but your name. Our marriage was under a tremendous amount of strain and I was afraid she'd take the baby and leave."

"Then when Katie was four months old she got a lung infection and was in the hospital. Her life was hanging by a thread. The chaplain came and asked us if we wanted prayer. He led us into a little chapel where we gave our hearts to God and committed our daughter's life into his hands."

Emma had been standing rigid watching the face that used to haunt her dreams, and knew that what he said was true. As she heard his story unfold her heart swelled within her chest, and compassion filled her eyes with tears. She knew then that she wasn't the only one who had suffered. Looking down at her hands she realized they had reached out of their own volition and she held them open palms up. Raising her eyes to his she said simply. "Her name was Angel."

Carl grasped her hands like a drowning man as she told him about the child he'd never known.

When she finished he asked her the question that had been burning on his heart for years. "Emma I know I have no right to ask this after what I put you through, but can you find it in your heart to forgive me?"

Emma's smile was sweet and she spoke softly. "Six months ago I couldn't have forgiven you if I'd wanted to. I was so wrapped up in bitterness that I was no good to myself or anyone else for that matter. Then God saved me and forgave me of my past. I can only do for you, what He has done for me."

As Jake watched he saw Emma free her hands and gently embrace the man who had over five years before ruined her life. Even from this distance he could hear Carl's quiet sobs as he and Emma cried together. Turning his head he wiped the tears from his eyes as he thanked God for what he had just witnessed.

"Daddy, Daddy!" Katie called as she spotted Carl releasing Emma. "Bring Miss Emma Daddy, I want her and Mr. Jake to walk with me, they know the song you sing to me at bedtime. Hey, why is everyone crying?" Katie looked around at all the tear-streaked faces. "Am I in trouble?"

Joe made an excuse about dust getting in their eyes and asked her a question about the pony she was riding, effectively distracting her from the situation taking place nearby.

Smiling Emma and Carl met Jake at the gate. As Jake's arm went around her Emma gave him a quick hug and her brilliant smile.

"Thank you Father," he breathed, hugging her back. Over Emma's head he offered Carl a tentative smile and stretched his hand out to him.

Carl watching Emma and Jake knew that this man loved her. He saw the trust and regard she had for him as she went uninhibited, into Jake's arms. With an astute eye he accepted the polite gesture and the men shook hands.

Carl asked Jake if he could have a word with him and they stepped away as Emma went to help with Katie.

"I'm Carl Robertson." He stated. "I met Emma once under bad circumstances."

"I know. Emma told us recently about her past. Although she mentioned no names I realized who you were."

"Oh, I see. I'm sure you would probably like to kill me right about now." The sad tones in his voice tore at Jake's heart.

"No, it took a big man to do what you've done today. I admire you for your bravery."

"I was drunk that night and when I realized what had happened I hated myself. I haven't had another drink from that day on. I've wanted to find Emma and ask her to forgive me for so long," he gestured helplessly. "I was hoping to tell her I'd gotten saved. I'm no longer the same man who hurt her. I can see how it is between you. I want you to know that I'd never done such a thing before and I certainly haven't done it since. I don't see how you can ever forgive me for what happened"

Jake spoke frankly. "At first, I'll admit, I wanted to hunt down the person who could have hurt Emma or any woman like that, and do- well, I'm not sure what I'd do to him. I knew something pretty bad had happened to her, but I didn't know what for sure until she told us. It took a lot of prayer, but I knew I had to let it go and forgive whoever had done this." Looking Carl in the eyes he said. "I forgave you when you were just a faceless attacker, and I forgive you still now."

Carl's voice was choked with tears. He took a deep breath and croaked, "Thank you. I don't deserve your forgiveness."

"None of us deserves it, but God places it in our hearts anyhow." Reaching out to shake his hand Jake felt as if a weight had been lifted from his heart. He knew beyond a shadow of a doubt that this was what he had been praying for. Emma was finally free.

Chapter 14

Emma stood watching Carl drive away with Katie. There were so many emotions running through her. Thankfulness that she had finally seen the other side of the picture. And sadness for the pain Carl would inflict when he told Cindy the rest of the story. He had insisted there be no more secrets between him and his wife. She was happy that everything was now out in the open. But the overwhelming freedom that coursed through her made her almost giddy. As if she had spun round and round until she could barely walk. She wanted to run and jump, laugh and cry all at the same time.

Turning she started walking faster and faster toward the river. The craziest, most "freeing" thing she could think to do was to jump from the swinging rope at the swimming hole, into the cold water.

Laughing she began shedding her hat, jacket and boots as she ran. When she reached the lagoon she took a firm grip on the rope and ran full force swinging out over the water. With a bloodcurdling war whoop she let go and plunged into the icy depths. As her head broke the surface, she gasped and shouted again. Laughing she saw Jake on the bank looking worried.

"Come on in, it feels great," she called splashing around to get warm.

Jake understood her feelings of elation; he was experiencing pretty much the same thing. Stripping down to his jeans he grabbed the rope and joined her. Shouting from the shock of the cold water, he splashed her for laughing at him and chased her round until he caught her laughing and kicking form. Emma's hands were splayed out over his chest and there was a merry light in her eyes as she struggled in his arms.

The slick moss-covered rocks were tricky to stand on and just when he thought he was on firm footing he slipped and they both went down. Sputtering he pulled her from the water where she clung to him wide eyed and grinning.

Without conscious thought he lowered his head intending to kiss her lightly but her lips met his halfway and lingered a moment too long and he was lost. All restraint was gone and he heard the wondrous sound of the walls they had erected these past weeks, crashing down around them. When their lips parted he had seen within her eyes the answer to the question he was afraid to ask as her love shone forth. Chilled and happy, they raced back to their cabins to take hot showers and get dressed.

Jake smiled at the loud music coming from Emma's cabin. He had heard only muted strains wafting on the breeze before, but today she was singing unrestrainedly along with it. There was such freedom in her voice. Jake couldn't help but sing with her. His heart was singing so loud that she must have been tuning in on the same wavelength.

When she'd hurried away from the corral he had followed at a discrete distance worried over what he might find. The last thing he'd expected was to see her swing uninhibited into the water. When he realized she was just blowing off steam, his relief had been so great, the next thing he'd known he was right beside her. The cold water had been exhilarating, but it hadn't held a candle to the victory kiss they had shared. How could she turn his freezing limbs into molten lava? Reminding himself to go slow he paused a moment for prayer before leaving.

Checking the time he went to Emma's cabin and knocked. The music was so loud he knew she would never hear him. Trying the door he found it unlocked. Cautiously he entered, not wanting to startle her. Turning the music down he called out to her. "Emma are you decent?"

"Yep. I'm right here." Walking out of the bedroom dressed in jeans and a sweatshirt, she flashed him her thousand-watt smile and laughed. "Jake Peterson, you look like you've been swimming. Now, don't you know that's a crazy, psychotic thing to do this time of year?"

"What can I say?" Slowly he walked across the room and stood so close to her, she had to tip her head way back to see him. "I'm not the only crazy, psychotic on the place." Smiling he threaded his hands in her hair. "Are you warm enough yet?"

Her breath caught in her throat as he deliberately brought his head down until his lips were an inch from hers.

"I could get a blanket," she teased as she raised her lips to his and kissed him lightly. "But then I don't think we need one." She murmured against his lips as her arms crept up around his neck and she gave herself up to his kiss. When she could breath again she suggested they collect the clothes they left by the swimming hole before someone got the wrong impression.

Grinning, he agreed.

He dropped her with a kiss at the kitchen door and headed for the stables.

"Was that Jake at the door?" Sue asked with exaggerated innocence.

"It might have been. I didn't notice." Emma returned in kind as she dropped her bundle of clothes on a chair.

"Oh come on Em, what happened? I heard something took place at the corral. Then Slim came in grinning from ear to ear and babbling something about 'skinny dipping'. Sue was bursting with curiosity.

"We were not 'skinny Dipping' we were fully clothed." Sobering, Emma filled her in.

"I can't believe it, Katie's father. That makes Katie, Angel's half sister. I can understand why you don't want anyone to know about it. It would only harm Cindy and Katie." Sue shook her head at the news then brightened. "Emma, I'm so happy, that part of your life is over now."

"I know Sue, I feel so free," she laughed. "I had to do the craziest thing I could think of, so I peeled off everything but my jeans and shirt, and jumped in the swimming hole." At Sues shocked expression she laughed and hurried on. "You should have seen Jake's face when he saw me in the water. I think he was trying to decide if I'd lost my mind. The next thing I knew, he'd jumped in too"

Giggling and holding her stomach Sue confided. "That may be one of the few crazy things I've ever heard of my brother doing. Since you've come here, Jake has come to life in a way I'd never have believed possible. I'm so grateful for you Emma. God sure knew what he was doing when he sent you here. It was even worth the broken ankle," she grinned.

"I don't know about broken ankles, but I do know about broken hearts." A reflective light glowed in Emma's eyes, "When I first came here I was broken beyond repair. Without God I still would be. Thanks for having a place where people aren't afraid to talk about Him, and He's an important part of everyone's lives." Emma carefully wrapped her arms around Sue and kissed her on the cheek.

Grinning and wiping tears they set about making lunch.

That evening Jake and Emma joined Joe and Sue in the great room. The central fireplace had been lit and the cozy atmosphere was just right for a quiet evening.

Sue eyed her brother with a twinkle in her eye. "I still wish I could have seen you swinging from that rope."

"Maybe you could join the 'Polar Bear Club' after you have Junior," teased Jake.

Throwing a pillow at him Sue grinned. "At least you didn't really skinny dip. I had to disillusion poor Slim. He was just guessing at what happened. He said he'd heard you two whooping it up and splashing, but he didn't want to intrude."

"See what you've gotten me into." Jake gave Emma an aggrieved look. "Now I've lost my tough guy image with the boys."

"I don't think anyone would believe you are a tough guy." Batting her eyes at him she continued. "I think you are really just a big teddy bear."

Joe dissolved into laughter. "Oh that's rich, you'll have to bring that one up at the next board meeting. 'Teddy bear Jake' initiating a cost efficiency inquiry of Hancock Hotels- "Ow! What'd you do that for?" Sue was giving him a disgusted look. "Oh no, don't tell me you still haven't told her yet."

Sue turned apologetic eyes on her brother. "The cat has already been let out of the bag. I'm sorry Jake, but I thought you told her in Nashville."

"Em, are you sure you want to let them know about your personal life?" Jake groused smiling. "Have the two of you divulged any more of my deep dark secrets?"

"Not that I know of. Do you have any more you want us to?"

"Not today I don't." Jake grinned. "Joe, what's on the books for tomorrow?"

"Gracie in the morning and that's it. With Thanksgiving next week things are slowing down. We really need that enclosed arena so we can keep the kids out of the cold. Were almost done for the season."

"I was thinking of taking a ride up to lookout point tomorrow. Anyone want to come along?"

"Thanks, but no thanks. I don't think a horse back ride would be a good idea at this stage of the game. We'll take a rain check in the spring." Sue held Joe's hand.

"I'm with her. Why don't you two go, you won't get another chance before the snow gets too deep."

"I'd love to," Emma yawned. "The view from there is beautiful."

"Okay we'll leave right after lunch. Be sure to dress

warm."

Joe rose and helped Sue out of her chair. "Come on, I'd better get you to bed young lady, you need your beauty sleep." He led a grumbling Sue toward their door. "Jake will you make sure the fire's banked?"

"I'm on it now," getting up, Jake banked the fire and adjusted the screens, and then he eyed a sleepy Emma. "Quote, 'I'd better get you to bed young lady.' Come on," taking Emma's hands he hauled her out of the chair.

"Do we have to leave the fire? It's so wonderfully warm."

"Yes, it's time to take you home. Here let me help." He zipped her jacket and turned up the collar. "Where's your hat?" Pulling her warm hat over her ears he dropped a kiss on her nose. "Ready?"

"As ready as I'll ever be. Where's your hat? It's my turn." Taking his hat and placing it firmly on his head she smiled and kissed him. "Let's go."

"Yes ma'am." Jake saluted.

Locking up they walked toward her cabin. The moonlight illuminating the scene made the flashlight Jake had brought unnecessary. They walked in silence her hand tucked firmly in his arm. Reaching her cabin he took her hand and turned her to face him.

"I'll see you in the morning." Tenderly he wrapped his arms around her and lowered his head brushing his mouth lightly over hers. "Goodnight my darling," he whispered and was gone.

Chapter 15

The air was crisp, but the sun felt warm on their backs as they rode along the trail up the mountain. Emma's memories came streaming back of the last time she was here. Summer was now gone for good and winter was settling in. Soon there would be more than the skiff of snow that had covered the ground this morning.

Emma had been worried that after last night's snowfall, Jake would cancel their trip, but nothing, it seemed, could dampen his spirits today. He was like a different man since meeting Carl. He seemed tender almost, well, unleashed. Her love for him had never seemed more intense then it did this morning. After the uninhibited way she had kissed him at the swimming hole yesterday, she had been afraid that he would withdraw from her again.

This morning he had been as friendly as normal, but with a slight difference. There had been a tender look in his eyes that made her want to declare her love for him then and there. The morning seemed to last forever and now they were finally alone.

Here at the higher elevation the snow was deeper. Grateful for the warmth of her heavy clothes, she noticed the hushed chill in the air as they entered the thick forest. Clouds of steam rose around them with every breath they took adding to the unreal quality of their surroundings. In the quiet atmosphere she prayed for guidance as she followed behind Jake. Watching his back as she rode, she found herself praying for God to lead him in all the many decisions he would face in his life. A song rose to her lips and spilled into the silence.

"Amazing grace how sweet the sound that saved a wretch like me, I once was lost, but now I'm found, was blind, but now I see."

Jake joined her and the words flowed between them as they emerged into the sunlight. God's creation spread before them as the sweet strains stilled. Snow lay heavy on the tree branches around them. Sunlight glittered off the snow making it look like millions of diamonds winking in the distance.

Dismounting, Emma helped Jake tie the horses. Then he swept the snow off the log and placed a blanket on it offering her a seat. Emma, who had brought the saddlebags with her, pulled out a thermos of coffee and poured them each a cup. Sitting with their hands wrapped around the warmth of the dark liquid they gazed out at the vista before them.

Breaking the silence Jake asked. "Do you know how scared I was the last time we were here?" As she shook her head in confusion he continued. "I wanted to tell you my testimony, but I didn't know where to start. I prayed all the way up here and as we were coming through the forest 'Amazing Grace' was on my heart. When you started to sing today, I couldn't believe my ears. I can't begin to tell you how much watching you gain your freedom has meant to me." Taking her hand in his he continued. "My biggest fear is that you won't need me anymore."

Looking into his eyes she saw the uncertainty and smiled tenderly. "Oh, Jake how can you say that? You led me to Christ on this very spot. Every time I slipped and fell you were there to point me to the right path. I know you have prayed for me. You've been a good friend to me, and I need you more now then you could ever know."

There was a sad light in his eyes. "Am I just a friend? Is that what our relationship is? Because if it is I'll need your prayers more than ever, you see Emma, I'm in love with you."

Emma's eyes filled with tears; unable to speak, she drew a deep tremulous breath as he rushed on quickly.

"I'm sorry, I've spoken too soon. Don't cry, I'll leave and not bother you again I don't want to bring you more pain." How could he have misread her? He had been sure he'd seen love shining from her eyes.

Emma's hand on his arm stopped him from rising. Slowly he turned to look at her. What he saw in her eyes had him gasping and dropping to his knees.

"Jake?" There was a question in her trembling voice as she fell to her knees with him. "I've prayed and prayed for God to either make you love me, or take this feeling away. I love you so much."

Wrapping her in his arms he tenderly kissed her as if she were made of glass then buried his face in her hair.

"Oh my love, my precious love." His voice shook with the force of his emotions. "Thank you Father for letting her love me."

Emma trembled in his arms their love a tangible thing she could feel all around them. Carefully he pushed her back onto the log, and brushed the snow off her clothes. His hand stilled on her knee as she covered it with her own. Looking up into the eyes he loved, with a deep breath and a prayer on his heart he spoke.

"Emma I can't begin to tell you what you mean to me. To know you love me is almost more than I can bear. I need you in my life." While he spoke he pulled the velvet bag from his pocket and holding it up so she could see the cross and the key dangling from the drawstrings, he explained. "When you told me to keep the key to your cabin it showed me you trusted me. I prayed every day that I would be worthy of that trust. When you were delirious with fever, you fought Carl in your dreams and even as I tried to comfort you I knew the pain was too deep. It tore me apart to know something so horrible had happened to you. While I held you and prayed, God showed me the gift of trust you had given me. I made a promise to him not to use this key, except for dire circumstances, until the day you became my wife." With the ease of much practice he removed the diamond ring and holding it out to her asked. "Will you marry me?"

Emma's eyes had filled with tears as he spoke; now they ran down her cold reddened cheeks as she breathed the one word he was waiting for. "Yes."

With a shout of exultation he jumped to his feet taking her with him. Picking her up he swung her around and around laughing and thanking God.

They startled a flock of birds from the nearby trees and they flew off in all directions. With her arms around his neck they kissed. It was a deep satisfying kiss with a promise of things to come.

"Would you please put this on before I lose it?" Jake asked loosening his hold on her and holding up the ring.

Pulling off her glove she held out her left hand, and with infinite care he slid the ring onto her finger and placed a kiss on it, sealing their promise forever.

"I was so afraid you didn't love me." They were once again seated on the log; she was snuggled against him with a warm blanket over their legs. Emma was content.

"Waking in your arms made being sick worth while," she revealed shyly. "Then when you were so shocked I was afraid you thought I was Amy."

"I knew exactly who was in my arms. It was you I kissed, no one else. I was afraid you'd be frightened." His face flushed, "I was dreaming of our wedding night."

"It must have been a powerful dream, because I felt it, and I was wide awake." Carefully threading her hands in his hair she pulled his head toward her punctuating her words with kisses. "I want to wake up in your arms every morning. I have never been afraid of you, only the intensity of my feelings for you."

It was some time before he put her firmly from him and announced with a sigh, that it was time to go. Gathering the blankets and saddlebags they repacked their things then walked back for one more look. They vowed to return in the spring when the warm sun would bring the wild flowers back in a riot of color.

Helping her mount her horse he checked that she was warm enough, and they started back through the forest. The lovely strains of 'Amazing Grace' ringing in the frosty afternoon air went with them.

Chapter 16

There was an air of hushed expectancy as Emma awoke. Today was one of the most important days of her life, her wedding day. Stretching luxuriously she prayed that everything would go well.

Tom Crowley the polite photographer from Nashville had arrived yesterday under strict secrecy, with Rebecca, his wife and partner. There would be no media circus at their wedding. Doc and Martha were safely in their cabin having brought the dress Emma had ordered. It hung now in her room. The veil hanging beside it she had made herself with the antique tatted lace her great-great-grandmother had made. The lace had graced the wedding veils of four generations of women, now Emma was to be the fifth.

Five, the number of grace, Emma smiled as she got up and readied herself for the day ahead, thankful for the grace that had changed her life.

The winter months at the ranch had flown by. They spent their days caring for the animals and working on renovations. Their nights were spent before the fire, fine tuning the plans for the ranch and wedding or working on their music. Little Joe Jr's arrival the eighth of January had them all in a panic at first, but he was a good baby and had settled in quickly. He had been the center of everyone's attention for four months and Emma especially adored him.

Today, Sue was in her element. The only thing that slowed her down was the cry of little Joe. Penny was acting as nanny while her mother, Mrs. Malone ran the kitchen.

The weather was cooperating beautifully and the warm April day was perfect. Ken had supervised the placing of six tall columns in the field of wild flowers off the terrace overlooking the river. White satin ribbons fluttered from the top of each pillar that the florist had carefully wrapped with garlands of wildflowers, ivy and baby's breath. Chairs, in neat rows marched down to the arc of pillars, lending an intimate while open setting.

Greg Paulson was overseeing the sound system and making sure the local DJ knew how to run it.

Tom wandered around snapping pictures of the preparations and Jake was everywhere. His nervousness evident, as he tried to make sure everything was perfect for Emma.

Joe finally found him in the kitchen showing an amused Mrs. Malone how to run the dish machine.

"Come on brother, we don't want the groom to have dishpan hands." Clapping him on the back Joe announced it was time for them to get dressed and led him away to the guestroom Sue had set aside for him.

"Are the boys ready? The ushers need to be on hand before we do." Jake stressed.

"Everything is on schedule. Ken has the boys corralled and I sent Susie off with Em, so quit worrying." Entering the privacy of the changing room, Joe locked the door and turned to his brother in law.

"There's only one place we can go to ready ourselves for what's ahead." Getting to their knees they approached the throne of grace to speak with their heavenly Father.

The camera flashed as Martha adjusted the veil on Emma's hair. Rebecca was staying with Emma taking pictures in the cabin, which they were using as the bride room. Standing back she took in the vision before her.

Happiness starred Emma's eyes as she posed for more photos. Her hair was the riot of curls Jake loved and the snowy white dress made her look like a princess. The scooped neckline and fitted bodice smoothed down to her small waist where the gathered skirt billowed to the full hemline.

Sue in a replica of the royal blue dress Emma had worn dancing, was radiant. Baby's breath and wild flowers tucked into her dark flowing tresses matched the bouquets she and Emma would carry.

"Em, Jake asked me to give this to you." Sue

handed Emma a small package. "He said you would understand."

Emma opened the velvet box and smiled sweetly. Tears threatening to spill over as she looked at the silver cross pendant and matching earrings lying on the bed of velvet.

Martha removed the heart pendant from Emma's neck and fastened the cross necklace in its place. As Emma changed her earrings she explained how he'd had the cross, tied to the strings of the velvet bag that had held her ring.

Cindy arrived with Katie and Gracie exclaiming over Emma's dress. Emma got to her knees to receive the girl's kisses. More pictures were in order and there were tears in Cindy's eyes as she hugged Emma. They had become fast friends and Katie was excited over the prospect of being the flower girl.

The time finally came when Doc arrived and sent the women to wait on the porch. Turning to his goddaughter he carefully placed his arms around her.

"Oh my dear, I wish your parents were here. They would be proud of you, just as I am." Taking her hands they prayed together before embarking on the journey that would change her life as well as her name.

Then it was time to go. Giggling and holding up Emma's skirt. The girls hurried to the Lodge with

Doc trailing behind. They took a moment to compose themselves as Cindy and Martha took their seats.

At the signal Gracie opened the door so Sue and Katie could begin their walk. Doc gently took Emma's hand and pulled it through his arm. Gracie helped arrange Emma's dress and shyly kissed her. Emma held her tightly and kissed her back, then she pulled a flower from her bouquet and tucked it into the little girl's hair.

The strains of Amazing Grace accompanied them down the isle as Joe held Jake's arm to keep him from hurrying out to meet them.

When the minister intoned, "I now pronounce you man and wife." Katie pulled on Jake's jacket and said in a clear ringing voice "That means you can kiss her." She blushed as laughter broke out followed by applause as Jake smiled and thanked her. Then he turned and tenderly kissed his bride. Music started and the recorded voices of Jake and Emma prayed as 'Tangled Hearts' followed them up the isle.

The reception was in full swing and the pictures were out of the way. The bride and groom circulated through the guests.

Emma could feel Jake's eyes upon her as she listened to Greg. "Emma, you have to be at the Music Awards 'Tangled Hearts' is sure to sweep the charts."

"I'll be there with Jake," she demurred. "He can receive the award for us and they have the recording of Tangled Harts."

"But, they don't want a recording, they want Jeri Forester."

"Are you harassing my wife on our wedding day?" Jake grinned as he shook Greg's hand.

"You talk to her Jake. It's time she came out of the shadows and received some recognition for her work."

"You've said that before, we'll pray about it," was all the assurance Jake would give him as he drew Emma away to the dance floor. "I don't know about you, but I'm about ready to leave." He whispered with a smile.

"Me too," she smiled. "Let's slip away and get changed."

Slowly they edged their way to the changing rooms and with Sue in tow they escaped.

Helping Emma out of her gown and stowing it and the veil carefully away, Sue kept up a string of chatter until Emma placed a finger on her lips asking, "what's wrong, what are you nervous about?"

"Was everything alright? I wanted it to be perfect." Sue wrung her hands tears filling her eyes.

"Everything was perfect, silly. I couldn't have

asked for a more beautiful wedding. I owe you and Joe so much, without your help I couldn't have pulled it off." Emma gave her a warm hug.

"That's what sisters are for." Sue sniffed. "Oh Em I have a sister!" She hugged her back.

Laughing, Sue answered a knock at the door and found Jake who slipped in and dropped a kiss on her cheek. "Susie can I have a moment with my wife?"

"Sure take your time." With a saucy grin she fled closing the door firmly behind her.

"Remind me to have a word with her husband when we get back home." Jake grinned as he held out his arms. Emma flew into them like a dove coming to roost.

"Home? Isn't this Joe and Sues home?" Her fingers toyed with his collar.

"The ranch is theirs, all but a certain cabin that I still have the key to. We can live here as long as we want or we can travel. Just say the word and we'll buy a house anywhere you want, as long as we're together." The skin where his lips were nibbling came alive with a fire they had diligently avoided these last months.

Trying to keep her sanity, Emma grasped at the first thing she thought of to distract him. "Shouldn't we tell Greg that we plan to sing at the awards ceremony?"

"Hmm, what?" His lips and hands were doing thing

to her nerves that her mind smiled at.

Laughing she pulled back, her mind was getting cloudy. "Pay attention to the matter at hand," she grinned kissing him back.

"I thought I was," he laughed. "Come on; let's get this over with so we can escape." He tucked her hand into the crook of his arm and headed for the door.

Scooping up her bouquet she followed happily. Emerging from Joe and Sue's apartment they came face to face with a line of couples waiting for them.

With a whoop, Slim wrapped Emma in a bear hug and gave her a resounding kiss, then passed her on to Romeo. Down the line she went laughing the whole way. Jake, after making sure she was not offended, joined in the fun and allowed the ladies to do the kissing.

At last, well kissed and not a little disheveled, she threw her bouquet. In the ensuing scramble Penny came up the victor. Proudly showing off her trophy, she colored prettily as Slim commented, "Way to go Romeo now all you need to do is catch the garter."

Red faced he joined in the good-natured jostling and with an unbelievable jump snatched the garter in mid air. Kissing Penny soundly he invited everyone to their wedding next month.

Amidst the ensuing confusion Jake and Emma left in a shower of rice. Waving out of the back of the limousine. They didn't get far. Just out of sight of the ranch house, Jake had the driver stop. Opening a compartment, Jake pulled out her jogging shoes and handed them to her.

"This is getting to be a habit," Emma teased. Remembering the night of the dance.

"Sue helped me this time," he explained as she changed her shoes. "She'll keep everyone busy for a while so we can slip back. The cabin is ready and we'll be able to hide out as long as we want, or at least until the food runs out." Laughing they gave the driver a wave and headed into the trees.

They quietly made a circuitous route to their cabin. Fishing the key from his pocket, Jake unlocked the door. He placed a hand on her arm as she started forward. Then he scooped her up into his arms where he nuzzled her neck in such a way that made her bones feel as if they were made of jelly. "Welcome home Mrs. Peterson." he murmured as he stepped over the threshold and kicked the door shut behind them.

Epilogue

Natalie Grey sat in her comfortable living room talking to her daughter on her cell phone. Ginny had called to make sure her mother had received the package she'd sent.

"Yes dear I believe it's all here, the pictures are beautiful. I'm sorry to have forgotten them. Thank you for sending them to me. Give my love to all. Good-bye."

Flipping through the photos she came across the one she had snapped of Jake and Emma that day at the airport. Smiling she remembered the encounter fondly. She chuckled over the memory of Emma's good-natured comment about never knowing what might happen.

Using the remote control she turned up the volume on the TV so she could watch her favorite show, Star Talk. Ah, she was just in time.

"This is Maria Turner reporting from the Music Awards. It was no surprise that 'Tangled Hearts' won big tonight receiving four prestigious awards. Including Best Single, Best Songwriter, Best Album and Best Artist."

"But, by far, the biggest surprise of all was when John Tabor joined his new wife, Jeri Forester, to sing 'Tangled Hearts'. There wasn't a dry eye in the place, mine included folks."

"Jeri Forester it turns out is the mystery woman John was seen dancing with last summer in Nashville."

"When the news of their marriage surfaced it was met with a wall of secrecy. These pictures have just been released, and as you can see it was a very beautiful wedding."

"Ms Forester won Songwriter of the Year and was just named Spokesperson for the Handicapped Children's Organization. All proceeds from the hit single 'Tangled Hearts' have been donated to fund a ranch for disabled children in the Colorado Mountains."

"Now that's what we call making a big difference. Congratulations Jeri and John on your marriage and any future ventures."

"This has been Maria Turner for Star Talk."

Smiling, Natalie once again looked at the photo she had taken at the airport. "You never know when you'll see a celebrity," she grinned.

www.ingramcontent.com/pod-product-compliance
Lightning Source LLC
Chambersburg PA
CBHW061142040426
42445CB00013B/1512